Gardens of Philadelphia and the Delaware Valley

Publication of this book, the third in a series celebrating the cultural resources

of Philadelphia & the Delaware Valley, has been supported by a grant

from The William Penn Foundation

Gardens of Philadelphia & the Delaware Valley

by William M. Klein, Jr.

Photography by Derek Fell

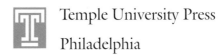
Temple University Press
Philadelphia

Dedicated to

F. OTTO HAAS

Chairman of the Board of the
Morris Arboretum of the University of Pennsylvania
from 1972 to 1988

Temple University Press, Philadelphia 19122

Copyright © 1995 by The William Penn Foundation

Photographs copyright © by Derek Fell

All rights reserved

Published 1995

Printed in Canada

Book design by Christopher Kuntze

This book is printed on acid-free paper for greater longevity

Library of Congress Cataloging-in-Publication Data

Klein, William M.
    Gardens of Philadelphia & the Delaware Valley / by William M.
Klein, Jr. : photography by Derek Fell.
        p.   cm.
    Includes bibliographical references (p.   ) and index.
    ISBN 1–56639–313–2 (cloth)
    1. Gardens—Pennsylvania—Philadelphia. 2. Gardens—Delaware
River Valley (N.Y.–Del. and N.J.)   I. Title.   II. Title: Gardens of
Philadelphia and the Delaware Valley.
    SB466.U62P485   1995
    712'.09748'1—dc20   95–16
                                                          CIP

Contents

Foreword

THIS BOOK represents the third and final in a series on the Philadelphia area's unique resources: its museums, public art, and with this publication, its gardens and arboreta. The idea for this book first took seed, appropriately, in the Wissahickon Valley. It grew out of an informal chat after a chance encounter between Bill Klein and me as we both were jogging from Harper's Meadow to Valley Green. Bill spoke enthusiastically of a concept he was developing about how American gardens evolved from originally walling out the wilderness to eventually walling out civilization 350 years later. I spoke of my interest in having the Foundation support a series of books for visitors and residents of the region celebrating some of the Delaware Valley's wonderful cultural assets. By the time Bill and I reached the covered bridge on Forbidden Drive, it seemed clear to both of us that a book on the region's gardens was a logical one for the Foundation series.

Most of the William Penn Foundation's grant resources are focused on breaking down walls and creating opportunities for those in our society who have been confronted with nearly impenetrable barriers—obstacles to a decent education, to jobs, health care, training opportunities, the list goes on and on. The fundamental mission of the Foundation is to improve life in the Philadelphia area, placing particular emphasis on empowering the neediest residents of the region. It supports programs that nurture families, promote social justice, strengthen communities, assist persons to participate actively in American democratic life, build a climate of cultural vitality and foster responsibility for our environment. This publication had been funded by the Foundation as part of its interest in encouraging the public's stewardship of our manmade and natural environments.

I hope that by discovering in this book the natural treasures of our region the public will become more aware of what exists here, that it will therefore more fully enjoy and appreciate our resources and develop a constituency to help preserve and protect them. Certainly, these special natural places in a rapidly urbanizing metropolitan region come to take on something of the quality of sacred sites. They are special sanctuaries of either engineered or natural harmony and beauty where one can find solace in a troubled world. These, as Bill Klein describes, range from the magnificence of vast cultivated landscapes to tiny urban parks in fractured inner-city neighborhoods. Each place is a special sanctuary for the people who know it.

That experience is described in the pages that follow; the reality exists in the real world beyond. After you read this book, go discover it for yourself.

HARRY E. CERINO
President
The William Penn Foundation

Preface

A RATHER LONG and winding garden path has been followed in bringing this book out. In 1981, in celebration of Philadelphia's 300th anniversary, the Morris Arboretum of the University of Pennsylvania published a guide to the gardens of the Delaware Valley in which the claim was made that this region contained the "largest concentration" of public gardens to be found anywhere in the nation. The idea was also advanced in this same publication that the region could, and indeed should, be regarded as "The Gateway to America's Gardens." In the intervening years, during which at least 20,000 copies of the guide were distributed, no one seems to have come forward to challenge these claims. And sometime in the mid '80s it dawned on me that through these gardens of the Delaware Valley, as nowhere else in the country, one could witness the evolution of our changing attitudes about nature.

Environmental issues continued to grow in importance through the decade. And as we were beginning to realize the implications of the federal and state rare and endangered species legislation many of our public gardens were beginning to see a new role for themselves. Places off the beaten path within our gardens were being restored to take on a natural, wild look. Pennsylvania's tercentenary celebrations had prompted a nostalgic look back, the field of restoration ecology was gaining momentum and recreating Penn's Woods in our various gardens seemed to fit well with the times. Nature centers and preserves encouraged by legislation that mandated environmental education were also beginning to sprout in many communities as the New Wave Gardens.

A botanist by training, who had strayed from the path of academia and systematic botanical research into garden administration, in 1986 I sat down at our kitchen table in the Price House in Chestnut Hill (the director's residence of the Morris Arboretum) to see if I could come up with a better way to present the gardens of the region. Undaunted by my lack of qualifications—as historian, horticulturist or landscape architect—I took on the project because I wanted to find a more coherent way of thinking about gardens. What I brought to that table was a background in the plant sciences, an appreciation for horticulture, an interest in history and, perhaps above all, a love for the varieties of gardeners who tended these special places.

Digging into the various gardens to identify their chronological and thematic development, I discovered that the more than forty gardens, parks and preserves could be grouped into seven major clusters—the chapters that make up this book. The earliest of these gardens were planted in the Colonial and Federal periods; the most recent appeared in the forms of nature centers and preserves. And within that 300-year time frame the gardens could also be grouped according to several major themes: collector's gardens, institutions for professional and avocational horticultural training, gardens as individual artistic expressions, the du Pont gardens of the Brandywine and public open spaces and parks.

Of course there are overlaps and inconsistencies in a design that attempts to accommodate such a diverse array of institutions: places such as the Awbury Arboretum that function as a community park and the Taylor Arboretum, managed by the Natural Lands Trust, treated here with preserves. But by thinking about gardens in a more comparative way trends could be identified—the earliest gardens, planted out of necessity and later transformed by imagination into artful spaces. And what wonderfully imaginative and varying leaps gardens take in the minds and in the spaces created by such contemporary garden artists as J. Liddon Pennock at Meadowbrook Farm, Arnold Bartschi at Swiss Pines and Sir John Thouron at Doe Run.

The du Pont gardens of the Brandywine, because of their scale, geography and what they tell about a gardening tradition in one family, stood quite apart from the others. They had to be treated in a chapter of their own. There are no published accounts of them collectively, and one that also describes them in relationship to the other gardens. And if ever there was an election for a "First Family of Horticulture" the du Ponts would certainly be among the top candidates.

Running throughout all of these gardens, but expressed in quite different ways and in differing degrees, is the irrepressible desire to increase the numbers and varieties of plants grown in a garden. But when a garden becomes a "collection" of plants it takes on other qualities—names, especially the scientific names, become important. The naming of plants is the province of the botanist or plant taxonomist. It requires an intimacy with the structures and functions of a given plant,

probing into its origins and defining relationships. And to the extent that the gardens become collections dotted with labels inscribed with Latin names they take on a scientific and educational purpose—they become arboreta (specializing in trees and shrubs) and botanic gardens.

The passion to collect was expressed early and strongly in Philadelphia through the travels of the Bartrams and Painter Brothers. It was a torch to be passed on to Mary and Josephine Henry (Henry Foundation), John Caspar Wister (Swarthmore and the Tyler Arboretum) and John and Lydia Morris (Morris Arboretum). Whereas curiosity motivated the quest initially, there is a growing sense of urgency today to assemble documented botanical collections as a hedge against the loss of the world's native flora. That growing sense of loss has been intensified by today's collectors who work at the boundaries of habitat destruction. They are bringing back an important message that is finding expression in these gardenscapes.

Embracing and sustaining these individual efforts, institutions grew up in the Delaware Valley to promote an interest in the culture of plants. The Pennsylvania Horticultural Society's production of the annual shows in the spring and fall has served as an intensive selection filter to advance our knowledge of plants and raise the standards of design and cultural practices. The Temple Ambler School of Horticulture, Delaware Valley College and the Barnes School have all contributed to a growing cadre of alums who promote a nurturing and sharing tradition through their communities. And there is no way of calculating the influence of a beautifully landscaped campus on generations of students who have walked the groves of academe at Haverford, Swarthmore and Bryn Mawr colleges.

William Penn's "greene Country towne" set the stage for the preservation of public spaces to protect the water supply and preserve the city's history. Rooted in the five squares of the original plan, Fairmount Park grew up the rivers and streams with the expansion of the city to become what many would regard as the city's greatest treasure. The "greene Country towne" was later to be enriched by a zoological garden, by several college campuses and by community parks. In the 1950s and 1960s the movement took on new energy and imagination in an effort to rescue the historic core of the city and create a national monument in the form of Independence Park.

The garden emerged for me over the decade of the '80s as a work of art or an invention always in progress. And like all works of art and inventions there is the passion to achieve some higher form of perfection—to order, to systematize and to control. I was to discover that the gardeners and the institutions they propagate operate on many different levels. There is the enthusiasm of the individual gardener discovering a new plant and the excitement in bringing it to flower and then to fruit and then to propagate it and begin the cycle all over again. To capture that enthusiasm for plants and gardening and transfer it to the next generation, however, requires organization and a fusing of diverse interests into a common purpose. Gardening in the Delaware Valley has become big business. And the Gardens Collaborative, created back in the late '70s as a consortium of garden-related institutions, was formed to celebrate & promote this gardening tradition.

My research assistant, Agatha Hughes, and I visited each of the gardens and walked and talked with the gardeners who had created them. At Pennsbury Manor I was taken by a demonstration of the different styles of fences used during the Colonial period. At Colonial Pennsylvania Plantations the worm fence, overgrown by weeds as it would have been during those times, zigzags across the fields tenuously holding back the great deciduous forest that presses down on this enclave. At Bowman's Hill Wildflower Preserve I discovered a lady slipper orchid growing in a wire cage in the forest. But it is at the John Heinz Wildlife Refuge at Tinicum where the message of 300 years comes home most forcefully for me. The chain link fence bounding this preserve strains to hold within it a threatened wetland habitat (water garden) that reverberates to the sound of highway traffic along I-95 and the comings and goings at Philadelphia International Airport. In 300 years we have come from fencing nature out to fencing nature in.

I also discovered, through reading authors such as Michael Pollan and Edward O. Wilson who were thinking along similar lines about gardens and nature, why we seem to be so powerfully moved by them. Before them naturalists such as Henry David Thoreau and John Muir had found a "garden," an Eden, in nature. But our world had proceeded beyond the point where distinctions between untamed nature or wilderness and tended space or gardens, had any real meaning.

Biological systems throughout the world are being dealt a devastating blow directly and indirectly through uncontrolled population growth and development on every front; no patch of earth remains untouched. And there seems to be no turning back. Conservationists and scientists now find themselves propagating native plants in nurseries and trying desperately to return them to their original habitats. Exotic weeds and other pests are being eliminated in preserves in favor of the natives. Planting and weeding, gardening activities, have now become the work of wildlife biologists. And so in the waning years of the 20th century the garden ethic is emerging as the most appropriate response for how we must view nature today. We must take a closer look at our gardens. There is a wealth of experience to be found in these special places that can, and indeed must, be more widely applied. And what better place to look than in Philadelphia and the Delaware Valley—"Gateway to America's Gardens."

For me this has been a labor of love through which I have personally rediscovered the garden as the place where we struggle to define our place in nature. And down this long and winding garden path I have also come to see the garden as metaphor for how we must view all of nature today—tended spaces where we collect, name, nurture and share our love of plants.

ACKNOWLEDGMENTS

This book opens for me in 1977 when F. Otto Haas, Chairman of the Board of the Morris Arboretum of the University of Pennsylvania, recruited me from the Missouri Botanical Garden. The Morris Arboretum grew and prospered under Otto's leadership through the '80s, and this book is in many ways the direct result of his unswerving devotion to Philadelphia and to the Morris Arboretum. And so it is to Otto, mentor and guide through twelve of my thirteen-year tenure as the Morris Arboretum's director, that I gratefully dedicate this book.

In 1986 the William Penn Foundation turned to Temple University Press to carry out a major publishing venture. And David Bartlett, Director of the University Press, challenged me to come up with a new conceptual framework for a book on the gardens of this region—a book that would be a suitable companion to the two other works that the University Press was publishing on museums and public art.

When I first spoke to David Bartlett about the project he had already begun to look into a few garden guides. He wanted the book to be substantive as well as beautiful. I introduced him to Derek Fell, the noted garden photographer and garden writer. Derek drew on his substantial library of photography and arranged to shoot many of the places that he had not covered before. Through Derek's images the variety and beauty of these gardens come alive.

I was midway in my career as Director of the Morris Arboretum by this time and had become somewhat familiar with many of the gardens in the area. I had also been around long enough to become a bit frustrated with the perceptions of our institutions and how a university arboretum had been marginalized by the academic community. "Write the book," David said. I was hooked!

My research assistant up until 1991, when I left the Morris Arboretum to assume the directorship of the Fairchild Tropical Garden in

Miami, Florida, was Agatha Hughes. This book owes much to her sense of order and the persistence she brought to bear on this project over a period of years while she also served as editor of the Morris Arboretum's Newsletter.

To my other colleagues at the Morris Arboretum this book also owes much. Timothy Tomlinson, Associate Director, Ann Rhoads, Chair of Botany, Paul Meyer, Chair of Horticulture and Curator throughout my tenure (now the Director of the Morris Arboretum), and Bob Gutowski, Extension Horticulturist, all contributed in direct and indirect ways. To the late John Hutton, director of Physical Facilities, and his successor Bob Anderson and a dedicated Morris Arboretum staff, who shared a vision of what could be, I extend my deepest thanks. This book is for you and for our colleagues at sister institutions who believed in the Gardens Collaborative and worked to bring it to earth.

The *Gardens & Arboreta of Philadelphia and the Delaware Valley,* that we published in 1981 blazed the trail we were to follow in creating a regional consortium of garden institutions. That publication was made possible through support from the McLean Contributionship, the Philadelphia Committee of the Garden Club of America and the Wilmington Garden Club. *Gardens of Philadelphia & the Delaware Valley* is the direct descendent of that modest little work and owes much to those who were there at the beginning of that enterprise.

Colin and Carole Franklin and the team of Andropogon Associates were the Arboretum's master planners, landscape architects and exhibit designers during the entire time I was director of the Morris Arboretum. This book has benefitted in many ways from our discus-sions and collaborations over the years.

It has also benefitted from my association as adjunct professor in the Biology and Landscape Architecture and Regional Planning Departments of the University of Pennsylvania and the collegial spirit I enjoyed with members of both of these departments. To Sir Peter F. Shepheard, former Dean of the Graduate School of Fine Art, Anne Whiston Spirn, Chair of the Landscape Architecture Department, and John Cebra, Chair of the Biology Department, I owe special thanks for their belief in what we were trying to accomplish: setting new standards for the academic garden.

The planning and production of four major flower shows in Philadelphia and London during the '80s played a significant role in my thinking about gardens. I would like to acknowledge here the contributions of colleagues at the Pennsylvania Horticultural Society, Longwood Gardens, National Botanical Garden, Smithsonian Institution, Royal Horticultural Society and the Royal Botanic Gardens Kew who produced exhibitions that gave substance to the Gardens Collaborative. In the process we learned something about the nurturing and sharing spirit of the garden. And while not specifically identified as such, the lessons from these international exhibitions can be found scattered through the pages of this book.

Elizabeth McLean, garden historian and a member of the Morris Arboretum Board, served in various leadership capacities in the production of the 1981 guide and as one of our several ambassadors abroad in coordinating activities on our major exhibitions. Elizabeth also cast her critical eye over this manuscript, made corrections and filled in many of the blanks that were left unresearched when I left Philadelphia. I am especially grateful for her many contributions to this book in seeing it through its final stages while I was off directing other gardens.

Special thanks are due to Caroline Seebohm, editor of this book and author of a number of her own garden books. Caroline managed to distill the essence of what I was trying to say while preserving my style and voice in the process. It was no easy job, perhaps more than she bargained for, but nevertheless she managed to do it and for that I feel a particular debt of gratitude.

Several garden friends who were influential along the way have now passed on to their heavenly estates: Adolph Rosengarden of Chanticleer, Harold Sweetman of the Jenkins Arboretum and Tom Hallowell of Deerfield. I am pleased that Chanticleer and the Jenkins Arboretum are represented in the book; Deerfield would have been included but unfortunately it is no longer open to the public. I am grateful that our paths crossed in the garden.

I've been exceptionally fortunate to have had several gardening friends and mentors along the way with whom I have shared some of the ideas of this book. Most prominent among these are Ernesta Ballard, former President of the Pennsylvania Horticultural Society, William Frederick, landscape architect and author, the late Henry McIlhenny, art connoisseur and the first Chairman of the Morris Arboretum's Fine Arts Committee, and J. Liddon Pennock of Meadowbrook Farm. They have contributed more than they will ever know.

A work that has spanned so many years I find incurs many debts along the way, but es-

pecially to those who believed in the original concept and were willing to see it through. Thanks to the Board of Directors, administration and staff of the William Penn Foundation for having the imagination and for being willing to invest in the publication of three books on the cultural resources of the region. And to Harry Cerino, Vice President for Programs of the William Penn Foundation, who thought that one of these three books should be on gardens. To David Bartlett I am especially indebted for his encouragement, direction and for keeping the project alive over these years and for lining up the capable book designer, Christopher Kuntze. All have invested themselves in this project and cared almost as much as I have in seeing it come out.

Finally, I would gratefully acknowledge my wife, Janet, a talented botanical artist who never lost her faith in me while serving as editor, critic, proofreader and mother of our four children: Darin, Jennifer, Melissa and Erica. My preoccupation with this book over the years ate into many early morning and evening hours, weekends, vacations and even time while recovering from heart surgery. In the meantime our children grew up in Philadelphia in the magnificent Price House in Chestnut Hill and somehow learned to suffer gracefully, even with good humor, "Dad's monomania" for plants and for turning every conversation into a discourse on plants and the garden. This book owes more to Janet and the Klein *kinder* than I can ever repay.

William M. Klein, Jr.
December, 1994

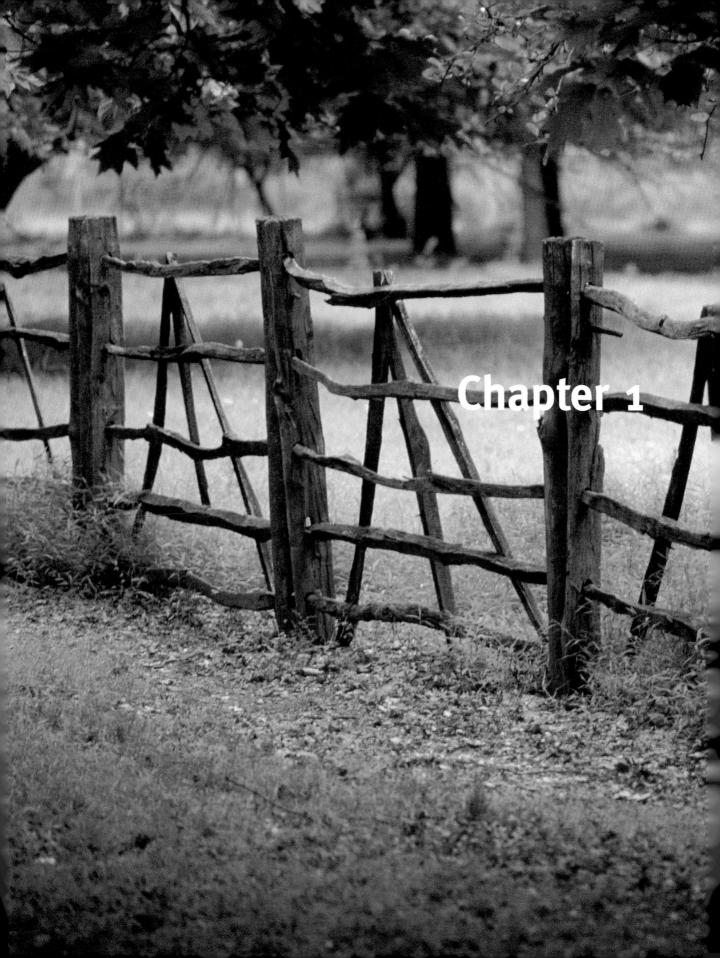

Chapter 1

Colonial & Federal
Farms and Gardens

Pennsbury Manor

By THE TIME William Penn arrived in Philadelphia in 1681, the area had been settled by Europeans for almost three generations. Dutch settlements dated back to 1609, followed by settlements of Swedes along the Delaware in 1637. The European population in 1681 was 2,000, and by 1765 Philadelphia had become the largest English-speaking city outside of London, with a population of 25,000.

The gently rolling hills and valleys of the 17th and 18th century countryside were covered with hardwood forest. Dominated by oak, chestnut and hickory, the forest was rich in species that could trace their ancestry back to relatives of the forests in Asia. Its most distinguishing feature is a dense green canopy in summer that drops its leaves to the ground in a blaze of glory in the fall.

Shielded by the Appalachian Mountains, the Delaware Valley has a relatively mild climate which, in combination with the fertile soils of the region, gave rise to a strong agricultural tradition. Mostly small farms, these outposts of civilization averaged about 200 acres and were carved out of the vast forests that pressed down upon them. The gateway to the American colonial garden was through the post-and-rail fence, frail lines of split rails that held back the monumental green wall of the Eastern deciduous forest. Within these fences, the colonial farms and gardens were the life-support systems that carried European agricultural and gardening traditions to the New World. They made the point that the first order of business in settling a new country was to provide for the necessities of life. They were the green machines that provided for the biological needs of their time.

In their kitchen gardens the colonists grew both savory and medicinal herbs side by side with fruits and vegetables for the household. These would have been supplemented by fruits, roots, leaves and bark—particularly those suggested by the friendly native Americans—collected from the surrounding woods. Some doctors, like Dr. Witt in Germantown, grew plants for their curative properties. Although created in the 20th century, the Physic Garden at Pennsylvania Hospital shows that close association between medicine and plant science.

The gardens of the 17th and 18th century inhabitants reflected contemporary attitudes about nature and science. As in the Mother Country, these gardens were

Andalusia

Colonial Pennsylvania Plantation

enclosed, rectilinear in design and informally planted. The fact that Philadelphia was founded by Quakers, and Germantown by German Pietists and Dutch Quakers, was to leave a strong imprint on the Delaware Valley. The Quakers—perhaps because they were denied outlets in music and the arts—had an appreciation of nature and an interest in natural science which was well ahead of their contemporaries. William Penn wrote that "the country life is to be preferred for there we see the works of God."

The dialogue with nature intensified during the 18th and 19th centuries as new regions of the world were opened by exploration, and technological advances in chemistry and optics made it possible to probe ever deeper into the causes and functions of life. The enthusiasm of the colonial farmers for finding new technology, introducing new crops and animal breeding can still be felt in the Delaware Valley gardens at Pennsbury, Peter Wentz's farm, Colonial Plantations and Andalusia.

Also emerging in these colonial gardens we see the impulse to transform gardens of necessity into gardens of art. A 17th century style garden has been recreated in the

Log Cabin at Stenton

Peter Wentz Farmstead

court in front of the Manor House at Pennsbury that clearly shows this desire to transform nature into predictable patterns. By the mid-18th century, several examples of a transitional style of landscape appeared: at the Penn family property "Spriggets-bury" (near present-day Lemon Hill), Richard Peters at Belmont and elsewhere. These combined "old-fashioned" elements such as topiary with garden statuary and vistas cut through the woods. No hint of these landscapes now remains. At Andalu-sia, Nicholas Biddle was likewise transforming his agricultural land into a park-like setting, an earthly paradise. Follies in the form of grottoes, and garden rooms where one could experience mysterious environments or simply enjoy the company of guests, were also created.

These forays into garden design were not the springboards to a new American garden style, but rather the American representations of long-established European gardening styles. This of course is not surprising when one considers that the col-onists were importing both plants and gardeners from Europe, Scotland and Eng-

Colonial Pennsylvania Plantation — a living museum

land. The largely transplanted European crops and agricultural traditions were over time tempered by American plants and American ingenuity, but the numbers of species of grains and vegetables grown in these colonial gardens were essentially the same as those in Europe at the time and even today represent only a small fraction of the plant kingdom.

It should be stressed, however, that alongside these European and English gardening traditions there was the deeply held belief that there was much in the natural landscape of the New World that was worthy to be introduced into cultivation. Foraging in the countryside yielded plants that were brought into the garden and later exported to England and Europe. The English particularly had an insatiable appetite for plants from the New World. The colonial gardens were the first stop on the way of a plant as it was shipped to England to be further refined. A number of such well-known garden plants as phlox, sunflowers and the "Michaelmas daisy" (actually an

improved variety of our New York aster, *Aster nova-belgiae*), became so closely associated with English gardens that we even think of them today as English garden plants.

Five of the seven gardens profiled in this chapter are associated with historic houses built by the founders of these properties. The existence of the house was in the majority of cases the rationale for preserving the historic site. Once the property was designated for preservation, it became apparent that the house had to be reset in the landscape and that meant that the garden had to be restored. With the large number of garden enthusiasts in this region there was no difficulty in finding some group to adopt the garden as a project. But once the excitement of restoration has faded, the true test of commitment comes in finding ways of continuing to maintain these precious sites. In combination, they tell a story of how fragile the garden is but also how persistent is our desire to have a garden, a desire that is as urgent today as it was when our colonial ancestors first carved out the ground.

OPPOSITE: *Pennsbury Manor*

Gardens of necessity into gardens of art

Pennsbury Manor

The country life is both the philosopher's garden and his library, in which he reads and contemplates the power of wisdom and goodness of God.

WILLIAM PENN

Transforming nature into predictable patterns

PENNSBURY MANOR was the country seat of William Penn, who in 1681 received a land grant from Charles II for a payment of £16,000 and founded Pennsylvania, Penn's Holy Experiment. The Manor House and gardens are a re-creation of 17th century garden styles, and the artisans and guides dressed in period costume animate this 17th century scene and make Pennsbury a must for every garden enthusiast and student of history.

An 8,000-acre forested tract of land was purchased by William Penn in 1682 from the Lenni Lenape Indians. By the following year, enough land had been cleared to start planting and construction on the Manor House. The fertile soil was the perfect substrate for the orchards, vineyards and gardens that Penn envisioned, bounded by the several styles of 17th century fence authentically reproduced here. The woods between the Manor House and river were cleared and planted with "hay dust" (grass seed) to open up a view to the river, with paths added for easy accessibility. The latter have been recreated with red gravel, as specified by Penn.

William Penn visited Pennsylvania on only two occasions for a total of about four years. But that he cared greatly about Pennsbury and wanted to oversee every detail of its development is borne out by the extensive correspondence with his agents and gardeners. Penn was a practical as well as a God-fearing man, and the first order of business in establishing his plantation was to provide for the necessities of life. "See we have a good kitchen garden," he wrote to his agent James Harrison in 1686. In keeping with that directive, Pennsbury Manor today has one of the most elaborate kitchen

"Set out a garden by the house," William Penn instructed his gardener

gardens to be found in the area. As many as 100 herbs and vegetables that are documented in Penn papers were grown in colonial times and can be found here, including roses, distilled for rose water, black currants, high in vitamin C, and greater celandine, used as a remedy for poor eyes.

"Set out the garden by the house, plant sweet herbs, sparragrass, carrets, parsnups, hartechokes, salatin, and all flowers and kitchen herbs there," William Penn instructed his gardener, Ralph Smyth, in 1684. As well as importing English plants and trees (peach, apple and pear were all grown in the orchards here with good results), William Penn was also well acquainted with the possibilities of

native plants. "It seems reasonable to believe that not only a thing grows best where it naturally grows, but will hardly be equaled by another species of the same kind that does not naturally grow there," he declared in 1683.

While much of life in colonial farms had to be spent on providing for essentials, the desire to bring to America those refinements of the garden so beloved by the English is very much in evidence. William Penn had a court garden set out on the Delaware side of the Manor House, which is planted today with many of the same plants that he would have enjoyed (including the tomato, which was admired for its fruit but considered poisonous at the time). Penn also made sure that the English garden

"Where a sweet place and retired is provided for thee and thine," William Penn wrote his wife

tradition was preserved by importing gardeners as well as plants.

His hope was that Pennsbury would one day become the family home. "I should think well of thy coming and living here," he urged his wife, Gulielma, back in England, "where a sweet place and retired is provided for thee and thine, this being the place God by his Providence has given to me and my offspring, and where is a fine people." But alas, Gulielma did not share her husband's enthusiasm for the country and for the privations of colonial life. In November 1701, having sunk many thousands of pounds into the property, William Penn returned to England, never to see Pennsbury again.

In spite of his best efforts to actively maintain Pennsbury from afar, the job was beyond him. By 1830 Pennsbury had fallen into a ruinous state, the orchards and gardens overgrown. Fifty years later, a movement developed to create a shrine or monument befitting the Proprietor. Pennsbury Manor was the logical place. The work of recreating William Penn's beloved estate was accomplished in the late 1930s under the direction of R. Brognard Okie, a prominent Philadelphia architect who had restored several important colonial houses. The garden was planned by Thomas Sears, a prominent Philadelphia landscape architect. Pennsbury Manor is now a state property maintained by the Pennsylvania Historical and Museum Commission, which has assured the public "that in Pennsbury Manor, as recreated, the great Proprietor's dream home again stands."

"See we have a good kitchen garden"

Vineyard

The centerpiece of this great Biddle family estate is the Greek Revival mansion with its monumental columned porch

Andalusia

The instinct of agriculture is for peace—for the empire of reason, not of violence—of votes, not of bayonets.

NICHOLAS BIDDLE

GRACIOUSLY SITED along the banks of the Delaware, Andalusia is located 15 miles upstream from Philadelphia in Bucks County. It has been the country seat for more than 170 years of the Craigs and Biddles. A legendary Philadelphia family, the Biddles were bankers, lawyers, politicians, military men, agriculturalists and gardeners.

The centerpiece of this great Biddle family estate is the Greek Revival mansion with its monumental columned porch. The 1806 building of Benjamin H. Latrobe was remodeled by Thomas U. Walter in 1835–1836. Both served as architects of the Capitol, Latrobe appointed by James Madison and Walter by Millard Fillmore. The Big House, as it is known, is furnished in the American Empire style and contains many family portraits and heirlooms. The grounds contain a number of other features of architectural interest: the Billiard Room (1815–1816), Gothic Grotto (1835), the Cottage and outbuildings.

This 19th century manor house takes maximum advantage of the view of the Delaware across a sweep of lawn punctuated by fine old trees. The placement of the billiard room and Gothic Grotto to enhance this view is a direct reflection of the English landscape movement of the 18th century. The 100-odd-acre estate is surrounded by natural woodland that preserves some of the few remaining acres of the forest that bordered rivers when the early settlers arrived in this country. The handsome walled garden, with the remains of the 1834 greenhouse scaled by wisteria and its beds separated by a billowing boxwood hedge, is of particular horticultural interest. The approach to the garden lies along the Green Walk, a contribution of the present Biddle occupant of

The Green Walk is a contribution of the present Biddle occupant

Andalusia reaches out to us in ways that history books never can

Wisteria draped wall at Andalusia

Andalusia and a demonstration of how the gardening instinct is passed from one generation to the next.

Andalusia is the vision of Nicholas Biddle (1786–1844). Biddle and his wife Jane acquired the property from the Craig estate in 1814, five years before his appointment as Director of the Bank of the United States. By 1830 Nicholas Biddle had become one of the most powerful and prominent men in the country. History books recount his struggle with President Andrew Jackson and the ultimate failure of his bank in 1841.

But Andalusia remains the living legacy of Nicholas Biddle and reaches out to us in a way that history books never can. It tells the story of the strongly held belief in pastoral ideals and how we must be good shepherds of the land. As early as 1822 Biddle chastised his fellow landholders about the way in which the land was being exploited. "Our farms . . . though small, are generally too large for our capitals; that is, we work badly too much ground, instead of cultivating well a little."

Nicholas Biddle devoted himself to his agricultural pursuits. His stables contained some of the country's finest horses. He introduced Guernsey cattle to the region and tried unsuccessfully to animate the silk industry by planting acres of mulberry trees. He retained his architect, Thomas U. Walter, to construct magnificent walls for his greenhouses, where he was able to raise fine grapes. The Biddles continued to harvest grapes from these vines until 1871, after which the greenhouses fell into ruin. Today the walls stand as a vivid reminder of how previous technology may be transformed by creative adaptation into art.

Andalusia has been a noble stage on which the Biddles created the legend of a great American family. Here we find in the Federal farm the desire to reach beyond simply producing sustenance to projecting onto the landscape the garden as a work of art.

The picturesque split-rail, worm fence tells the story of how the hardwood forests of the region were cleared

The Colonial
Pennsylvania Plantation

It was decided to recreate
a working family farm as it existed during the
Revolutionary War Period and to use this farm
as a research and educational center.

BISHOP'S MILL
HISTORICAL INSTITUTE

The 18th century well-head as theatrical stage

STEP BACK to the 18th century and meet Joseph Pratt, an English Quaker farmer, and his family. Plantation staff and volunteers plough the fields with horses, cultivate the garden with 18th century tools, harvest the crops, cook on a great open hearth, spin fiber into thread and weave and sew their own clothes.

The Colonial Pennsylvania Plantation was part of a 1686 William Penn land grant of 300 acres to Thomas Duckett. The farmhouse was constructed in 1705, and the period being interpreted here is from 1760 to 1790. From nine to fifteen members of the Pratt family would have lived here. The technology was simple yet ingenious. One can sense the rigors of life in the New World, the unpredictable nature of the seasons and the careful husbanding of resources.

The picturesque split-rail worm fences tell the story of how the hardwood forests of the region were cleared. Today these fences keep red Devon cattle, Dorset sheep and a pair of draft horses from straying—animals that would have felt right at home on a colonial farm. If these fence rows and pastures have an untidy appearance, the look is authentic. Some of these pastures have never felt the plough, and the lawnmower is still 65 years into the future. The grass is cropped here by animals, the scythe or not at all.

The kitchen gardens of this period contained a variety of herbs and vegetables growing in raised beds. All the plants served a practical purpose, including *Calendula* (pot marigold) for food coloring and wormwood (*Artemisia absinthium*) as a moth repellant and bandage. The crops harvested in the fall were placed in root cellars, the 18th century answer to refrigerators and the lifeline between harvest seasons. The garden as art would have been an unimaginable luxury in such places. The people here earned their living the old-fashioned way—by the sweat of their brow.

On the way to the farmhouse there is a pigpen with long-snouted, primitive-looking animals. The 18th century pig was a cross between domestic and wild varieties and was allowed to run at will on these plantations. In the fall a shock of flax may be seen drying in the field. It takes several years from field to garment. You can see today the inhabitants wearing clothing produced on the plantation.

The Colonial Pennsylvania Plantation is now a 110-acre working farm managed by the Bishop's Mill Historical Institute, established in 1973 for the purpose of building the Plantation as a Bicentennial project. More than ten years later, we can now experience the benefits of this experiment in colonial living and also see how our museums are being transformed into theatrical stages in order to bring their stories to life.

BELOW: *The 18th century pig was a cross between domestic and wild varieties*

*The kitchen gardens of the period contained
a variety of herbs and vegetables*

From 9 to 15 members of the Pratt family would have lived here

"Serve me faithfully, as thou expects a blessing from God, or my favor, and I shall support thee to the utmost as thy true friend."
WILLIAM PENN TO JAMES LOGAN

Stenton

*I can hardly help telling thee how
beautiful my venerable mansion looks
with its vegetation in full glory. . . .*

Deborah Logan (1781–1839)

An exquisite brick manor house on three and one half acres in Germantown, Stenton has been authentically restored to the period of 1730–1830. The buildings (with the exception of the early 18th century log house which was moved here in 1968) are original to the site. In an adjoining building there is a rare example of an early orangery dating to about 1769. Dominating the view to the left of the entrance is a stone bank barn filled with period garden implements and dating to 1787. Otherwise, the rough-mown grass and a few fine old trees are but faint reminders of the original landscape.

Stenton was the country seat of James Logan (1674–1751). The original property, purchased by Logan in 1714, covered an area of 500 acres. James Logan had come to this country in 1701 as a secretary to William Penn. He served Penn faithfully and became a major political force during the first half of the 18th century. He was a man in the Renaissance tradition, statesman, writer, scientist and philosopher, and served in various capacities as Secretary of the Governor's Council, Mayor of Philadelphia, Chief Justice of the Supreme Court and Acting Governor.

James Logan was an intellectual; his belief in a higher being and interest in technological innovation were typical of the Quaker founders of the Commonwealth. His knowledge of the Lenni Lenape language allowed him to negotiate treaties with the hundreds of Indians camped on the fields surrounding Stenton. He was drawn to all kinds of scientific inquiry, and his experiments on the sexuality of plants were praised by the Swedish botanist Linnaeus, who had produced one of

Eighteenth-century log cabin moved to Stenton in 1968

the earliest and most widely used systems of plant classification in 1735.

This fascination with plants was passed down to his son William, who went on plant-collecting expeditions and built the orangery to winter over his lemon trees and tender plants—an 18th century application of solar technology to the propagation of non-hardy plants. James Logan's grandson, George, also inherited the family passion for horticulture, which was well augmented by that of his wife, Deborah Norris Logan. George received his training as a physician at the University of Ed-

inburgh, but when he returned to Philadelphia in 1780, he devoted himself to agriculture and the improvement of farming practices. It was George Logan who brought a "pretty appearance" to Stenton and introduced park-like lawns and a new carriageway. Jefferson refers to George Logan as "the best farmer in Pennsylvania." George Washington occupied Stenton in August of 1777 during the Revolutionary War, and returned ten years later to see firsthand the state-of-the-art agricultural practices that he might later apply at Mount Vernon.

The visitor today must be prepared to summon up some imagination in order to appreciate what this landscape must have been like when James, William and George Logan occupied these grounds. In the middle of a densely-industrialized section of the city, Stenton now stands as a lonely reminder of the past. But it holds a seminal place in the history of this country, dispensing the accumulated knowledge of European culture and alive with inventive minds aimed at establishing traditions and far-reaching innovations that would distinguish their new land. The many contributions of James Logan and his wife Deborah to Philadelphia were acknowledged in 1825 when one of the parks established in the original plan of the city was named Logan Square.

The house has been lovingly restored and managed since 1890 by the National Society of the Colonial Dames of America in the Commonwealth of Pennsylvania. Between 1910 and 1915 Logan's descendant John Wister, a name that we associate with the Scott Arboretum, designed and installed the boxwood garden, planted principally with shrubs and flowers known to have been grown by the Logans. The garden is being restored; when completed it will add a measure of garden interest as well as making a statement about the Colonial Revival period in landscape restoration. The property is owned today by the City of Philadelphia. In 1965 Stenton was designated a National Historic Landmark.

Georgian architecture, commanding the "High Lands" over the picturesque Wissahickon Creek

The Highlands

The whole estate is a striking example of science, skill, and taste applied to a country seat.

TURNING OFF Sheaff Lane in Montgomery County onto the grounds of The Highlands, we leave suburbia and enter the rural landscape of the late 18th and early 19th centuries. The entrance road gradually inclines to the manor, a fine example of late Georgian architecture, commanding the "high land" over the picturesque Wissahickon creek that gives this historic house and garden its name.

The Highlands was built as the country home of Anthony Morris, son of Samuel Morris, who commanded with distinction the First Troop of Philadelphia City Cavalry in the Revolutionary War. Anthony Morris had acquired this 300-acre tract of land (now 43 acres) in 1794 and completed The Highlands two years later. A member of a distinguished family, he was a lawyer by training (class of 1783 at the University of Pennsylvania), an international merchant and importer, President of the Pennsylvania Senate and at age 27 the first Speaker of the House of Representatives. A close friend of James Madison, he is credited with having introduced him to the widowed Dolley Payne Todd, whom Madison later married.

The Highlands grew out of Anthony Morris's desire to have a country estate to live and entertain in as befitted a gentleman of his position. It was designed as a *ferme ornée*, an elegant landscape combined with a working farm. The manor house has a view of Morris's elegant spring house, and the original gothic smokehouse and privy bear witness to Morris's taste. The demands of such a property and lifestyle however proved too much, and Morris sold The Highlands in 1808. In the advertisement for the sale of the property, the land's virtue for agricultural purposes was stressed.

George Sheaff planted many of the fine old trees and constructed the crenelated wall that enclosed the garden

The architectural outlines of today's garden can be traced back to George Sheaff, a wine merchant and prominent citizen of Philadelphia who acquired the property in 1813. He planted many of the fine old trees that are still on the site and constructed the magnificent crenellated wall that encloses the garden to the north of the Manor House. Grapes were espaliered against this wall, with gothic garden house and gardener's house framing it at either end. In 1844 Andrew Jackson Downing made no mention of Sheaff's garden but admired his productive and aesthetic landscape.

The estate remained in the Sheaff family until 1915, when Miss Caroline Sinkler ac-

quired it. By that time the garden had gone through several cycles of decline and rejuvenation, but the basic outlines were still intact. With the help of prominent Philadelphia architect Wilson Eyre, Miss Sinkler created an elegant new garden within the Sheaff framework. The Morris smokehouse and privy became garden houses; the George Sheaff greenhouse was torn down, its back wall enclosing the garden on the south. A boxwood garden, herbaceous beds, grotto, pergola and statuary were additional refinements, and wisteria was trained up George Sheaff's grape wall.

The Sinkler period (1917–1940) brought The Highlands to the pinnacle of gardening

perfection. During these years The Highlands was frequently visited by famous architects and horticulturalists, and was described in magazines and journals as one of the finest gardens in the country. In 1933 Caroline Sinkler received the Pennsylvania Horticultural Society Gold Medal for creating this masterwork. In 1940 she sold The Highlands to her niece and husband, Mr. and Mrs. Nicholas G. Roosevelt. The property was gifted by the Roosevelts to the Commonwealth in 1957 and conveyed to the state in 1970. An estate auction in the 1970s dispersed much of the Sinkler statuary.

According to some authorities, The Highlands started its decline when it became part of the Commonwealth. However, in 1975 The Highlands Historical Society was formed to maintain the garden and raise funds to support the place. The Society proceeded to hire architects, Fred Peck and George Patton, to assist in the restoration of the property. The Society has approved a master plan by Andropogon Associates, Ltd., to restore the property in a way that will reflect its 200-year history, so that The Highlands may return once again to the elegance of the great country seat envisioned by Anthony Morris.

A kitchen garden may have caught George Washington's eye as he looked down from the corner bedroom

Peter Wentz Farmstead

George Washington slept here.

GEORGE WASHINGTON occupied these premises in October of 1777 when he was preparing for his campaign to re-engage the British after his defeat at Brandywine. To deserve such a notable presence, the farmstead of Peter Wentz (1719–1793) must have been one of the better known and more comfortable farms in the area.

Located in Worcester Township, Montgomery County, the Peter Wentz Farmstead maintains the pastoral character of the original setting. The property included 300 acres, of which 90 acres are maintained here today. Horses and sheep graze in pastures bounded by worm fences. An orchard has been established to recreate this ubiquitous feature of the colonial farm. The centerpiece of the landscape is the Georgian-style farmhouse built by Peter Wentz, Jr., in 1758. This solid fieldstone house, with its roof across the first story, shows German influences in such details as the bright colors.

The earliest record of a member of the Wentz family in Montgomery County is 1713. Peter Wentz's father was a privateer, that is, someone who has a license to return stolen goods for a profit. The property came under the control of Peter Wentz, Jr., in 1744, the same year the barn was built. Relatively little is known about the Wentz family, although there was an inventory of the householdings at the time of Peter Wentz's death in 1794. The furnishings of the house have largely drawn upon this inventory.

The most characteristic garden element and the focal point for horticultural interest is the German-style four-square kitchen garden. Carefully researched by the Norristown

The focal point for horticultural interest is the German style, four-square kitchen garden.

Horses and sheep graze in pastures bounded by worm fences.

Georgian-style farmhouse built by Peter Wentz Jr. in 1758

Garden Club, the kitchen garden guide currently includes 85 plants and classifies them according to whether they were grown for culinary, medicinal, fragrance or landscape purposes.

As in the case of the Colonial Pennsylvania Plantation, the gardens of Peter Wentz's Farmstead are practical, and the urge to transform the utilitarian garden into an art form seems to be expressed only in the selection of plants grown for the purposes of delighting the eye or appealing to the sense of smell. The closely-cropped lawns indicate that present-day managers have yielded to current technology in the form of the power mower, a machine unknown to the colonial farmers, who would not have recognized the tidy appearance of the grass. (This neatness, however, might well have appealed to the original family's German sense of order.)

Peter Wentz's Farmstead was acquired by the Montgomery County Commissioners in 1970 and is maintained today by the County as an historic park. Costumed guides and volunteers add greatly to the atmosphere of the period. As is the case in many historic houses, there are activities throughout the year to make the period come alive, including arts and crafts, blacksmithing, broom-making, spinning, tinsmithing and weaving. The Farmstead is clearly in the process of moving from historic house to living theater.

Twenty-five per cent of the prescription pharmaceuticals on the market today are still derived from flowering plants

Pennsylvania Hospital
Physic Garden

The delight [in plants] is great but the use is greater and joined often with necessities.

from GERARDE'S *Herball* OF 1597

PHILADELPHIA WAS an early center for medicine, and so it should come as no surprise to find the idea of a physic garden proposed in colonial Philadelphia. Adam Kuhn, a native of Germantown and a student of Linnaeus in 1761, was appointed in 1768 the first professor of materia medica and botany in the College of Philadelphia (University of Pennsylvania). In 1774 the managers of Pennsylvania Hospital received a proposal to establish a botanical garden on the grounds. The proposal was enthusiastically endorsed, but it took 200 years and the impetus of a Bicentennial celebration finally to get the job done.

Located on the grounds of Pennsylvania Hospital at 8th and Spruce Streets, the Physic Garden displays the wide range of plants that were grown in colonial times. The garden, with its elevated beds, is laid out in the familiar quadrant pattern, surrounded on two sides by plantings of 26 kinds of trees and shrubs that have been carefully selected for their medicinal properties. Seventy-seven other herbaceous plants are grown here—everything from *Aconitum* (Monkshood) for toothache and sciatica to *Viola* for pulmonary problems, relief of pain and reduction of inflammation.

While many people come to admire these wonderful displays for their color, shape and scent, they may regard the medicinal properties of the plants with some skepticism. It may come as a surprise to learn that 25 percent of the prescription pharmaceuticals on the market today are still derived from flowering plants.

It is fitting that a physic garden of such note should be located on the grounds of Pennsylvania Hospital. Chartered in 1751, this

was the first hospital in the colonies, and justifies a visit in combination with the Physic Garden, to explore these connections between medicine and plants. The hospital contains the first medical library of this country, established in 1835. It is a treasure chest for bibliophiles and contains many of the references used to research the plants found in the medicinal garden.

While the concept of the physic garden is an ancient one, visitors should keep in mind that this one is new, dating from 1976. The garden has a lushness to it that reflects modern propagating techniques and aesthetics. (No pesticides, however, are used.) The Physic Garden was made possible by the energy, imagination and persistence of the ten member clubs of the Philadelphia Committee of the Garden Club of America and Friends of the Hospital, whose members maintain the gardens and provide information to interested visitors.

The Pennsylvania Hospital Physic Garden invites us to explore these connections between medicine and plants

Chapter 2

The Collector's Garden: Recreating Eden

Franklinia alatamaha at Bartram's Garden, named in honor of Benjamin Franklin, was first discovered by the Bartrams along the Alatamaha River in Georgia in 1765; it was last seen in the wild in 1803

OVERLEAF: *Morris Arboretum*

WHILE COPERNICUS managed to put the sun in the middle of the celestial universe in the 16th century, God held the central position of man's universe in the 18th century and well into the 19th. According to the Genesis account, God had created the heavens and the earth and on the sixth day He created man and placed him in a garden. The good news that came down through the 18th century was that these acts of creation were the products of a rational God; this meant that the mind of God could be comprehended by the mind of man. The bad news was that He also created unpleasant things in the garden of Eden such as thistles, poisonous plants and invading armies of weeds. But it was thought that even these seemingly wanton creative acts might have been performed to test the wit and ingenuity of man and thereby increase wisdom.

The collecting of natural history objects, their description and their illustration thus became a matter of following in the footsteps of the Creator. The plants could be brought back and cultivated in gardens, these recreated Edens, to add further insight into what the Almighty had in mind. Everything had a purpose, and the 18th century collector's garden was the machine created to advance that purpose. The gardens of John Bartram and the Painter brothers, for instance, can be thought of as offspring of those 16th century botanic gardens of England and Europe which were designed to reassemble the acts of creation that had been dispersed after the Fall of Man.

To understand the importance of John Bartram (1699–1777), one must recognize the passionate interest in exploration and collection of plants that obtained during his lifetime, an interest that was driven by the need to provide a rational scheme for God's diversity. John Bartram became interested in plants at an early age, and although he lacked a formal education (he was raised by his grandparents, his mother having died young and his father having been killed by Indians in the Carolinas), that curiosity led him to take Latin from a local schoolteacher, Latin being the language of science. He acquired copies of Linnaeus's system of classification from James Logan of Stenton and proceeded to try to place everything he found into that system.

Bartram possessed both the intellectual energy and the physical stamina to undertake strenuous expeditions, where he collected plants and seeds and brought them back to grow in his garden. But his great contribution was his ability to disseminate his finds amongst the rest of the world, which was hungry for his discoveries. It is

Bartram's Garden

Painter Brother's Tyler Arboretum

said that hardly a ship left Philadelphia during those times without a consignment of plants or some other natural history objects: snakes, frogs, butterflies or whatever, and much of these exchanges with the colonies came about thanks to John Bartram's energy and resources.

There was an enormous demand in England for anything from the New World. The mid-18th century was a very active period in the development of what we know today as the English landscape school, a main characteristic of which was sweeping vistas of naturalistically planted groves of trees (a fine example of which is Stourhead, the masterpiece of Henry Hoare, created in 1741). In the badly deforested country that England had become, this appetite for large numbers of trees, coinciding with an interest in North America, meant that it was possible for American plantsmen to enlist wealthy patrons who were willing to invest a few guineas each year to underwrite the expenses of travel and shipping of plants. Fellow Quaker and London mercer Peter Collinson, for instance, Bartram's friend by correspondence for 35 years, became Bartram's unpaid agent to eventually over 100 clients—one of whom planted 10,000

Dr. Joseph Kassab's Wallingford Rose Garden

Belvedere at the Morris Arboretum

American trees in one year alone. Collinson also introduced Bartram to Dr. John Fothergill, the noted London physician, whose name we associate with the Physic Garden of Pennsylvania Hospital and who was probably the first to have a section of the garden set aside for North American plants, the so-called "American Garden."

John Bartram also found the time to enrich the intellectual life of Philadelphia and was co-founder with Benjamin Franklin in 1743 of the American Philosophical Society. He was rewarded for his efforts during his own life by the patronage of notable people and the esteem of the scientific community. In 1765 he was appointed King's Botanist by George III, and given an annuity of £50. It was characteristic that the first payment of this award was used to take the expedition to Georgia where he and his son William discovered the *Franklinia*. To George III, who presided over the loss of a Crown colony, we also owe some measure of gratitude for saving a lovely plant. It was a German botanist, Hedwig, however, who in 1789 named a genus of moss *Bartramia* in Bartram's honor. In so doing he gave Bartram the kind of immortality that botanists regularly bestowed upon one another.

But of all the honors that were bestowed on John Bartram, none could have been more satisfying than to have his interest in plants passed on to his son William. John Bartram fathered eleven chldren by two marriages, and nine of these children, seven of them by his second marriage to Ann Mendenhall, survived into adulthood. But it was to William that he transmitted his curiosity in the world of plants. "My little botanist," John Bartram refers to William, and it was to him that he passed the lamp of his botanical genius.

William Bartram (1739–1823) had the soul of an artist. Accompanying his father on expeditions, he spent much of his time drawing plants. He had his father's eye for discriminating plants and took copious notes of all the species that he could identify. His writings contain many of the original observations on the Indians as well as on the geology, soils, streams and vegetation.

Into everything he saw, William Bartram read the works of the Creator. He saw in the bald eagle "tyranny," in the dove, "fidelity," and in the native American Indians, hopeful signs of character that would allow them to be brought peacefully into the white man's culture. He returned from his travels in January 1777, six months before his father died, and settled down to the task of writing up his travel records in a book published in 1791. In a decade the book went into nine foreign editions. *The Travels of*

Hybrid Lilac at Tyler Arboretum

William Bartram through North and South Carolina, East and West Florida is a classic. Carlyle wrote Emerson about its having a "wonderful kind of floundering eloquence." It also inspired the poets Samuel Taylor Coleridge and William Wordsworth to borrow images from it for their poems, and thus contributed to the beginning of the Romantic Movement in English literature.

Like the Bartrams, the Painter brothers, whose lives spanned the first 75 years of the 19th century, were Quakers and deeply interested in plants. They became the prime movers in the creation of the Tyler Arbore-

Tyler Arboretum in apple blossom time

tum. Minshall Painter was the more outgoing of the two brothers. He showed an early interest in natural history, collected plants, minerals and insects, and made systematic meteorological observations, some of which were sent on to the Smithsonian. He demonstrated an aptitude for tools and, according to one report, was convinced by his mother that he should stick to farming. But even down on the farm he managed to maintain an active interest in the affairs going on about him and was one of the founding members of the Delaware County Institute of Science.

Jacob, the more retiring of the two, had a particular interest in language. With his brother, he spent much of his time reading in the library, writing and printing his writings on his own printing press. Their interest in the world about them was encyclopedic and in their writings one gets the full force of the 19th century belief that it is possible to come to grips with the facts of the world, categorize those facts and even predict outcomes. They lived in a world that was committed to rational thinking. Together, the two brothers created what they referred to as a Cycle of Knowledge, that

places knowledge into sixteen categories ranging from "Faculties of Consciousness" to the "Absolute." Clearly the Painter brothers, Jacob in particular, are the intellectual descendants of scholars who, two hundred years before, tried to create a universal language.

It should come as no surprise that two minds so occupied with the classification of natural history would want to collect trees and shrubs and place them in common culture for study; in short, create an arboretum. But it is in the library, surrounded by the telescope, microscope, printing press and manuscripts of the Painter brothers that one feels most strongly the passion these two Quaker farmer-scholars had for their pursuit of knowledge. They appear here as the embodiments of Alexander Pope's dictum: "Slave to no sect, who takes no private road, / But looks through Nature up to Nature's God."

William Carvill's work reflects a more extrovert approach to man's relationship to the landscape than that of the scholarly Painter brothers. Carvill was English, and his basic plan for the Haverford campus was inspired by the English school of landscape gardening, which is so strongly associated with the names of William Kent (1686–1748), Lancelot (Capability) Brown (1715–1783) and Humphry Repton (1752–1818). The choice of the open "natural" landscape style instead of the walled gardens of Oxford and Padua tells us something about the desire to establish a different kind of dialogue with nature.

Most gardens can trace their success to the work of a relatively few individuals who have managed to turn their passion for plants into a life's work. The campus gardens at Swarthmore and the Scott Arboretum are examples of this commitment by John Caspar Wister, the offspring of a prominent Philadelphia family. (The climbing plant wisteria was named for a 19th century member of another branch of the family.) Wister's prodigious appetite for plants was already apparent at the age of 14. He grew up in Germantown and graduated from Harvard in 1909, taking a degree in landscape architecture. He worked for another prominent Philadelphia landscape architect, Thomas Sears, from 1912 to 1913, and his name is associated with several other gardens in the Delaware Valley, notably Stenton and the Tyler Arboretum, where he served as director from 1946 to 1965. He wrote many influential books and was a founding member of the Iris Society. When Arthur Hoyt Scott (1875–1927), son of the founder of Scott Paper and a Swarthmore alumnus, started the A. H. Scott Horticultural Foundation in 1929, John Wister became the first director. He remained until 1969, bringing his talent to bear in establishing nurseries, introducing new horticultural varieties on the college campus, setting up a "plant infirmary" and providing a framework for plantings based upon botanical groupings. Swarthmore students were able to walk out of their classrooms and through a time machine back to the very beginnings of seed plants.

But John Wister understood that the garden had to have more than simply an intellectual framework. It must be beautiful and transport the visitor into a world of fantasy. Screening plants of evergreens were used to provide that unity of design he was looking for. The woods were cleaned up and planted to feature native plants. He built his botanical castle of many rooms, featuring his own and Scott's favorite plants—irises, peonies, daffodils. He insisted that the campus should not be regarded as a "plant infirmary," but that collections had to be constantly evaluated and culled in order to arrive at new and better varieties. The quest for Eden had ended with Darwin.

Not all the pioneer gardeners were men. In the tradition of Bartram's garden, the Henry Foundation started in the late 1920s as an outgrowth of the personal enthusiasm for plants of Mary Gibson Henry (1885–1965) and her daughter Josephine de N. Henry, born in 1911. Mary Gibson, whose husband was a prominent Philadelphia physician, was influenced by William Robinson's book, which encouraged the use of native plants. Over a 40-year period, she managed to undertake 90 collecting expeditions and died on her last trip in 1967 to North Carolina.

Mary Henry's collecting was not what one would call systematic. Like Bartram, she was a seeker after new species. She was a keen student of plants, with highly-developed observational skills, but not a professional botanist or horticulturalist. Her collecting was undertaken at times in a chauffeur-driven car, although she also knew the hardships of the field. Her collecting interests ran to the unusual: albino forms, darker foliage, double flowers and plants that expressed unusual vigor. She felt a particular attraction for genera such as *Styrax*, *Lilium*, *Helesia* and *Rhododendron*, and was particularly interested in finding southern plants at the northern limits of their ranges,

Mary and Josephine Henry's Foundation for Botanical Research

something new that just might be hardy in Philadelphia. Her sharp eye led her to discover two new species, *Lilium iridollae* and *Chamaecyparis henryae*.

Fortunately, the passion for collecting plants passed from Mary Henry to her daughter Josephine, who could hardly wait until she graduated from Agnes Irwin School to accompany her mother on collecting expeditions. Together they would occasionally encounter life-threatening situations, such as being held at gunpoint in 1940 when they accidentally came upon a moonshiner while collecting in North Carolina. Josephine also tried to find a *Styrax* collected by her mother in Texas, instead coming home with another trophy, *Lilium michauxii*, previously known to grow only in the southeastern states. Thus the Henry Foundation is a garden of plant trophies and an intensely personal assemblage of plants by two intrepid plant collectors.

Another woman who made a lasting contribution to the gardens of the Delaware Valley was Elisabeth Philippe Jenkins, daughter of B. Pemberton Philippe. Her love of nature and gardening may have been inherited from her ancestor Israel Pemberton, Jr., a prosperous Quaker merchant who in 1747 purchased Clark Hall on Third and Chestnut Streets, which was described as an attractive residence with formal gardens. When Elisabeth Philippe married H. Lawrence Jenkins, who had been an invalid since his service in the British merchant marine in World War I, her father built for them a large stone house with a 20-acre tract, and from 1929 onwards until her death in 1964, Elisabeth transformed her passion for nature into an extensive garden and bird sanctuary.

A passion for roses informs the garden created by the late Dr. Joseph Kassab and his wife Betty. The Wallingford Rose Garden boasts hundreds of different varieties of rose, in a setting of rare and native trees. Like the Henry Foundation and the Jenkins Arboretum, this landscape is inscribed with a signature just as personal as those signing the Declaration of Independence.

The relationship between a teaching collection, dominated by scientific ways of thought, and a collection of plants originally assembled for their aesthetic value is a complex one. The struggle between the garden as an art form versus the garden as a collection became an all-out institutional issue at the Morris Arboretum, which was originally the country estate of the brother and sister of a large old Philadelphia family, John T. Morris (1847–1915) and Lydia T. Morris (1849–1932).

Jenkins Arboretum

Using the best Philadelphia architects, including Stewardson & Cope, Robert McGoodwin and Theophilus P. Chandler, the Morrises built a country home and carriage houses called Compton on 29 acres of the 175 acres that now make up the Morris Arboretum. They collected furniture and furnishings of the highest quality for the house, many examples of which are now in the Philadelphia Museum of Art.

They made six voyages to Japan, India, Alaska, Russia, Europe and Egypt between 1881 and 1906, and brought back ideas from the gardens they visited and transplanted them onto the landscape in Chestnut Hill. Japanese garden styles held a particular fascination. John Morris employed a Japanese landscape gardener to construct one of the early authentic examples of Japanese landscape and rock design in this country. Italian stonemasons were readily available in Philadelphia, and the terraced gardens with balustrades, the rose garden and the orange balustrade reflect the Italian and French influence. The seven arches which head the English park remind one of the arches of the great William Kent landscape at Rousham Park in England. The grotto under the Mercury Temple is an echo from the great 1741 Henry Hoare land-scape, Stourhead. "Victorian Eclecticism" has been the name given to the garden style of these variously collected elements, and the Morris Arboretum is one of the most complete examples to be found anywhere in this country.

Both John and Lydia Morris wished to establish a natural history museum that would contain the objects they had spent a lifetime collecting in their travels around the world. In founding the Morris Arboretum, they were able to achieve their dual objective of escape from the world of encroaching urbanism they saw around them and the establishment of an educational institution that would reach down to future generations. Along with Compton, the Bloomfield property, a working farm when it was acquired by the Morrises in 1913, was an integral part of that vision to create a center for educational activities, for training young people in how to grow plants and preserve their environment.

After John Morris died in 1915, Thomas Sovereign Gates, President of the University of Pennsylvania, persuaded Lydia Morris that the educational objectives she and her brother sought could best be carried out under the administration of the University. Thus in her will, along with instructions about the scientific laboratory she wished to see on her property and the broad public agenda she wished carried out in the form of lectures, books and pamphlets on scientific investigations into horticulture, she stated that Compton and Bloomfield shall be known as "The Morris Arboretum of the University of Pennsylvania." Since her death in 1932 many famous botanists and naturalists at the Morris Arboretum have made major contributions to the study of horticulture.

Each century must have its own explanation for how the world operates. The 18th was the Age of Enlightenment, and the Bartrams and Painters, with their intellect and their discerning eye for biological form, were in tune with that age and made major contributions to it. The Quaker philosophy that informed the gardens of their successors continued to make nature approachable as the manifestation of God, enhanced by the 19th and 20th century commitment to education through scientific horticultural scholarship.

OPPOSITE: *Morris Arboretum of the University of Pennsylvania*

A gathering place for notable plants, politicians and scientists during Colonial times

70

Bartram's Garden

*It is God Alone Almyty Lord
the Holy One by Me Ador'd.*

1770 inscription
by JOHN BARTRAM
on his house

BARTRAM'S GARDEN is America's oldest surviving botanical garden. It occupies a 44-acre tract of land in West Philadelphia along the Schuylkill River. It is here that European traditions of science took firm root in the natural genius of John Bartram (1699–1777) and his son William (1739–1823). As a garden, it was a gathering place for the notable plants of North America, many of which went on to find their way into European gardens. It was also the gathering place of the notable political and scientific figures of colonial times. Delegates from the Constitutional Convention gathered here to take a break in their proceedings on July 14, 1787, and to see the treasures of the plant world that had been assembled by America's first native-born botanist.

This property was acquired by John Bartram in 1728 for the sum of £40. The house and gardens were molded to reflect John Bartram's view of the world and its Creator. (A devout Quaker, he was an independent thinker, however, and was read out of Meeting for not believing in the divinity of Christ.) For the botanically uninitiated, John Bartram's garden would have appeared untidy, overgrown and lacking in those qualities of design and structure that we have come to associate with the garden as an art form. George Washington, who visited in 1787, admired the curious plants but said the garden "was not laid out with much taste."

Today, the colorful display garden of Bartram-period annuals and perennials planted on the side of the house facing the Schuylkill would probably be more pleasing to General Washington. Bartram's Garden is known more for its notable trees and shrubs, however, than

Black Maple in Fall

for its flower beds. There are many fine old specimens, including a large ginkgo, introduced into this country from China in 1784. The yellowwood (*Cladastris lutea*) near the house is a particularly ancient specimen; the heartwood yields a yellow dye. There are two magnificent specimens of buttonwood (*Platanus occidentalis*) down the slope from the house; this species is one of the parents of the London plane tree. The large oak to the right of the entrance on the opposite side of the house from the Schuylkill is referred to as Bartram's Oak. Its scientific name, *Quercus heterophylla*, derives from the variable (*hetero*) forms of its leaves (*phylla*). The oak was an apparent hybrid found by John Bartram growing on the property when he bought it.

But of all these notable specimens, the one that has been most closely identified with

"Perhaps there is not any part of creation, within the reach of our observations, which exhibits a more glorious display of the Almighty Hand, than the vegetable world." WILLIAM BARTRAM

Bartram's Garden is the *Franklinia*, a member of the tea family (*Theaceae*) which includes the genus *Camellia*. It has become the signature of this garden, the genus commemorating the Bartrams' close friend, Benjamin Franklin. Plants of this genus were first sighted by the Bartrams in 1765 along the Altamaha River in Georgia near Fort Barrington. Seeds were later sent back by William Bartram on his trip to that same area in 1773. This was fortunate, for the plant was last seen growing in the wild in 1803.

The garden, based upon a sketch plan drawn in 1758 by John Bartram, is undergoing restoration to bring it back to its original design concept. The trees were originally planted in rows, as one would expect in a collector's garden where plants are grown primarily with the object of study in mind. The fences are also being restored to their original positions, materials and style.

The buildings, which fortunately have been very well preserved, originated in colonial times. The central portion of the house dates back to 1689, when the property was owned by Swedes. John Bartram made several additions to the house during the time he lived there. His initials and those of his second wife, Ann Mendenhall, are carved in the southeast (gable end) of the house with the date 1731. In 1770, at the age of 71, he undertook major renovations to the facade, erecting three columns carved of native stone and constructing the second-floor sitting room and bedroom. After the British defeated the colonial army at the battle of Brandywine in 1777, John Bartram, fearing the British would "lay waste his darling garden, the nursling of al-

Cider Press along the Schuylkill River

the 44 acres that now make up Bartram's Garden were bought by the City of Philadelphia under the auspices of the Fairmount Park Commission. The non-profit Bartram Association manages the property, and since 1979 a new masterplan by Rudy Favretti has been produced for the garden, programs have been expanded and comprehensive and authentic restorations have been undertaken, focusing on the years 1728 (when Bartram first acquired the property) to 1823, the date of the death of his son William. It is on the National Registry of Historic Places and in 1985 was designated by the Secretary of the Interior as the John Bartram's Garden Trails, a component of the National Trails system.

most half a century," stayed close to home and died here on September 22, 1777.

The interior of the house is mostly restored and refurnished to portray the colonial lifestyle, with authentic furniture and pieces donated by members of the Bartram family. The outbuildings include the seedhouse where John Bartram processed the seeds and plants from his various expeditions. Many are now classrooms and accommodate an active educational program run by the Bartram Association, which was founded in 1893.

In 1850 Andrew Eastwick, a self-made engineer and inventor, who was retained by the Czar of Russia to build the trans-Siberian railroad, bought Bartram's Garden, which he had admired as a boy. He tactfully built his house on the neighboring property, leaving the garden as a pleasure ground. In 1891, at the urging of Thomas Meehan, Eastwick's gardener and a well-known Philadelphia nurseryman,

The outbuildings, barn and stable, now accommodate classes for an active educational program

"A correct classification of facts is instructive, for it teaches the affinities and distinctions among things." JACOB PAINTER

Tyler Arboretum

From Nature's Laws He Drew his Creed

as Taught by Nature's God.

Jacob Painter

THE FAINT echoes of 18th century rationalism still resonate in the giant sequoia, ginkgo and cedar of Lebanon, which were planted by Minshall and Jacob Painter. The Tyler Arboretum, located in Lima, Pennsylvania, reflects the passion for collecting of these two Quaker farmer-scholars.

The 700-acre arboretum is underlaid by three geological formations which have given rise to a diverse topography, mantled in woodlands of oak, tulip poplar and beech, and interspersed with meadows and grassy knolls. Twenty miles of trails bearing such names as Dismal Run, Rocky Run, Dogwood and Pink Hill (named for the mountain pink *Phlox subulata*, which are in full flower in late April) penetrate the natural woodlands.

The Tyler Arboretum borders the 2,600-acre Ridley Creek State Park, and together these properties form one of the region's largest and most valuable holdings of land maintained in a naturalistic forest state. Along the paths of the Tyler Arboretum more than 380 species of plants of the Pennsylvania flora have been identified, and the checklist of birds lists 164 sightings. Walking these paths one can still glimpse, if ever so faintly, nature as experienced by the colonists.

The Tyler Arboretum is part of a 1681 land grant to Thomas Minshall, who arrived in Pennsylvania in 1682 with his wife Margaret Hickock. The property remained in the Minshall family for eight generations. Minshall Painter (1801–1873) and Jacob Painter (1814–1876) inherited 500 acres of the original 625-acre landholding from their father and started planting from the 1830s through 1875. Neither brother married; they remained

In the 1950s and '60s extensive rhododendron plantings were established

serious students of natural history their entire lives.

The Painter brothers planted more than 1,000 trees, with seeds from Robert Buist, the John Evans Arboretum and the Hoopes Brothers Nursery. About 20 of those trees are still growing, and are among the largest of their kind known on the East Coast. The giant sequoia, now almost 80 feet tall, was planted between 1856 and 1860 and has become the living symbol of the Tyler Arboretum. Approximately 200 acres have been carved out of this landscape to be managed for the purposes of collections. The remnants of the historic 19th century Painter Brothers Arboretum lie to the east of the barn and manor house.

The Tyler Arboretum was named for John J. Tyler (1851–1930), nephew of Minshall and Jacob Painter. After the Painters died, the property became overgrown and deteriorated. John Tyler was an admirer of his uncles, and at his request, a 68-acre arboretum was established to honor their memory. Upon the death of his wife Laura Hoopes Tyler (1859–1944),

A "Cycle of Knowledge" in a circle of cypress knees

the property was placed under the administration of a board of Trustees, with John C. Wister as director from 1946 to 1965.

Wister in his meticulous way set about researching the history of the Painter brothers, defining their intentions and cataloguing their plants. He made extensive inventories of the properties and extolled the promise that this property holds. He grappled with the issue as to whether this should be in fact a managed collection or allowed simply to become a natural park or preserve, a struggle continued to this day.

In the 1950s and 1960s extensive rhododendron plantings were established along with magnolias, maples, crab apples, hollies and conifers. A fragrant garden designed and maintained by the Philadelphia Chapter of the Herb Society of America was planted in 1940, and a bird habitat garden was planted in 1981 at the entrance to the John C. Wister Education Center.

No trip to the Tyler Arboretum would be complete without a visit to the historic buildings, including Latchford Hall (1738), and the greenhouse where the Painter brothers kept their non-hardy plants, which has now been restored and is used for propagating plants for sale. The barn, which was constructed in 1833, has also been restored and now carries the name of the John C. Wister Education Center, a fitting memorial to one of the area's most ardent plantsmen and horticulturalists.

A suitable setting for the "guarded education" that a group of 19th century Quakers were seeking for their sons

Haverford College Arboretum

A pleasant, elegant and spacious landscape that complements the surrounding community.

WALLACE, ROBERTS & TODD, landscape architects

TURNING OFF Lancaster Avenue one leaves the Main Line suburb of Haverford to enter a 216-acre campus arboretum. With its scattered groves of trees in open meadows, playing fields and a duck pond that doubles as a skating rink in winter, the Haverford campus reflects the design of the famous landscape at Stowe, in England. The resemblance is no accident.

Haverford College was established on the present site in 1831. In 1835 William Carvill, an English gardener, was hired to create a campus landscape that would be a suitable setting for the "guarded education" that a group of Quakers were seeking for their sons. The gently undulating hills, woods and streams provided the perfect canvas on which the ideals of Quakerism could be painted, and also reflect Carvill's sympathy with the English landscapists, whose visions he borrowed for the New World.

Although Carvill's garden plots are long gone, the Quaker ideals of community can be seen in his groves, which were laid out in the area now called Barclay Beach. In his original plan Carvill had specified seventeen plantings of trees, alternating balsam fir with yellow buckeye, Lombardy poplar, black locust, sugar maple and tulip poplar. The groupings consisted of seven trees, all of the same species, arranged in a pattern with six trees in a circle and a seventh tree in the center. A remnant of one of these groves remains, showing the symbolism of the arrangement—a community (in the circle) with the individual truth-seeker preparing for a life of service in the center.

The perimeter of woodland was planted in 1924 and gives the campus a sense of closure

The William Penn Treaty Elm lives on in its fourth generation at the Haverford Arboretum

Some of the finest specimens of their kind to be found in the area

which adds to the feeling of community. A 50-acre pinetum was established in 1926 and is now being catalogued and upgraded. The core of the campus is made up of a series of interlocking quadrangles. An interpretive brochure provides a listing of 100 notable trees in this area of the campus. Many of these are the finest specimens of their kind to be found in the area: Osage orange (*Maclura pomifera*), dogwood (*Cornus florida*) and Hinoki false cypress (*Chamaecyparis obtusa*). Typical of the Quakers' sense of fair play, less than half of these trees are natives, the majority being introduced species or representatives of hybrid origin.

The killing winter storms of 1902 that eliminated many of the trees on the campus mobilized the Campus Club (founded a year earlier), and members gave their support to restoration plans produced by John S. Cope. In 1907 Samuel Parsons, in association with the well-known nurseryman, Samuel C. Moon, developed a plan for renewing the campus landscape. In 1911 Thomas Meehan & Sons were retained to enlarge and enrich the plantings. Some of their work can still be seen along the nature walk that traverses the woodland. In that same year, the dread disease of chestnut blight came to the area, and by 1921 all of the chestnut trees on the campus were gone.

Thanks to the Frances J. Stokes Fund (established in 1919), R. J. Johnson was hired after this catastrophe to produce a plan for the landscape, and this plan, effected in 1926, formalized the idea of an arboretum by setting aside 50 acres for a generic collection of conifers. Today, the Pinetum (recently named the Ryan Pinetum in recognition of volunteers Richard and Nancy Ryan), covering an 18-acre tract near the southwestern border of the College, boasts 300 trees. The Dutch elm disease struck in 1948, but through all of the devastation wrought by the disease, the William Penn Treaty Elm, now in its fourth generation, lives on.

Memorials have enriched the landscape, such as the Mary Newlin Smith Garden, designed by John Cope, a tribute to a gardener and college matron; the Woolman and Strawbridge Groves; Dougherty Memorial Terrace; and the Tubb Fund of the Class of 1925. Endowments by Edward Woolman and the names of Oakley and Wylie are also associated with efforts to restore, replant and maintain the character of this landscape.

The Haverford College Arboretum Association was founded in 1974 by Stevenson W. Fletcher, who arrived on the campus in the mid-50s. The Association oversees the maintenance of the collection and a number of programs, some of which are designed to involve the student more directly in the maintenance of the landscape. In 1974 the Campus Beautification Program was revived, and in 1980 a nursery was established.

In 1984 the College retained the Philadelphia firm of Wallace, Roberts & Todd to undertake a master plan. A model planning document was produced, giving directions for how to preserve the original elements of the Carvill plan while adding new elements which will maintain the unity of the architectural features and the distinctiveness of the living collections.

Trees planted in a circle to symbolize community with the one individual truth seeker at the center

These groves of academe grow from the belief that gardens and landscapes impress values on students and the community

Scott Arboretum
of Swarthmore College

It is good for college students as well as for the general public in and near a college town, to learn the beauty of hardy outdoor plants.

JOHN C. WISTER

THESE GROVES of academe are located in Swarthmore, west of Philadelphia. The entire campus of Swarthmore College, an area of 330 acres, of which 150 acres is in woodland, is maintained as a curated collection of trees and shrubs, an arboretum. It is a collector's garden par excellence and a model of what a university college campus should aspire to.

The Scott Arboretum was officially launched in 1929, with the establishment of the Arthur Hoyt Scott Foundation for Horticulture. Scott, son of the founder of the Scott Paper Company and a member of the Swarthmore class of 1895, was a founding member of the Iris Society but had a particular fondness for lilacs. In fact, he had traveled to New York to see lilac trial gardens and became intrigued with the notion that there should be a place in the Delaware Valley where gardening enthusiasts could come to see the best plants that could be grown in this area. In 1925 Professor of Botany Samuel C. Palmer presented to the college administration the outlines of their joint plan to develop the college campus as a curated collection of plants to serve the dual purposes of beautification and education.

Today, the Swarthmore College campus numbers among its collections over 5,000 kinds of trees and shrubs representing more than 200 woody genera. Its collections of lilacs, peonies and hollies have been assembled to represent the best that this region has to offer.

For the most part, John C. Wister designed these gardens. Over the years the work of other distinguished landscape designers has also been represented on the campus: Thomas McCabe (for whom the amphitheatre is

Collections are constantly evaluated and culled; this is not a "plant infirmary"

named), Harry Wood, Thomas Sears, William Frederick and George Patton. Throughout all this development, John Wister remained true to the original inspiration which created this campus garden.

The record of accomplishment at the Scott Arboretum would not be complete, however, without reference to John Wister's wife, Gertrude, a distinguished plantswoman in her own right and also Assistant Director of the Scott Horticultural Foundation from 1955 to 1962. She came to Swarthmore in 1940 and is the author of a number of publications, among them *Hardy Garden Bulbs*. She is the recipient of many honors and awards and in 1985 was awarded the A. H. Scott Garden and Horticulture Award, 55 years after her husband had received the first one.

OPPOSITE: *A curated collection of plants to serve the dual purpose of beautification and education*

Mary Henry sought her quarry in the remotest regions of their range

The Henry Foundation for Botanical Research

The uniqueness is found in the superior quality of the individual plants accommodated upon the grounds.

JOSEPHINE HENRY, 1986

Many are the rarest forms of the species they represent

PROTECTED FROM bulldozers and the destructive forces of development, the garden of the Henry Foundation is located off Stoney Lane in Gladwyne, Pennsylvania. It is the outcropping of two eminent Philadelphia plantswomen, Mary Gibson Henry (1884–1967) and her daughter, Josephine de N. Henry (born 1911), who inherited her mother's passion for collecting plants and who has made her life's work the perpetuation of both the spirit and substance of this collector's garden.

The Henry Foundation started as a 105-acre farm. Today, the garden covers an area of 40 acres of steeply sloping land with a picturesque outcropping of metamorphic (gneiss) rock. Like many gardens of this region, this one grew out of a lifelong interest in plants that can trace its beginnings to the late 1800s when Mary Henry was growing up. It wasn't until 1927, however, that she began to fan the embers of her passion into full flame and create a collector's garden.

The garden of the Henry Foundation contains many rare forms of the species they represent. Some of these plants, such as *Itea virginica* "Henry's Garnet" and *Berberis x gladwynensis*, have been introduced into other gardens. Among the plantings, the visitor will also find Mary Henry's "species of eternity," *Phlox henryae* and *Lilium mary henryae*. Many, such as *Magnolia ashei*, are treasures from collecting expeditions over a 40-year period.

After her death in 1967 while on a collecting trip to North Carolina, it was left to Mary Henry's daughter to undertake the long and arduous process of sorting out her mother's gardens and cataloguing her vast collections.

Phlox henryae *and* Lilium mary henryae *are Mary Henry's "Species of Eternity"*

Plantings are placed where Mary Henry thought they would do best

It is a monumental undertaking that is still going on today.

The handsome Norman English house on the property was built in 1926 and contains a library of approximately 1,000 volumes which are accessible upon request. The Foundation was formed in 1948 to preserve native plants from Canada to Florida and west to Texas, New Mexico and Montana. The garden has been open to the public since 1974.

True to the spirit of the collector's garden, Mary Henry "never grew a plant that she could buy"

White Wisteria at the Henry Foundation for Botanical Research

Enter this rose-decked operating room of the late Dr. Kassab through the hedge of Alberta spruce

Wallingford Rose Garden

Our current mission is to provide interested visitors with an opportunity to see a private garden maintained by its owners in an everchanging design.

MRS. JOSEPH KASSAB, 1986

Scattered throughout the grounds are many specimens of unusual trees

TWO MILES south of Media at the southeastern corner of Brookhaven Road and State Highway 252 (Provident Road), garden enthusiasts will find roses in training, blooming and being recycled in a totally innovative fashion.

The house, which is situated near the center of this 4-acre property, was built in 1887 by Simon Gratz, a prominent Philadelphia educator, who constructed the home for one of his daughters. The rose garden dates from the early 1900s, when a Philadelphia chemist, Edwin Rosenbluth, laid it out not so much as an aesthetic design but for scientific purposes, and started his experiments with sprays to control pests of roses. The present owner, Mrs. Joseph Kassab, acquired the property in 1941 with her late husband, Dr. Joseph Kassab. Dr. Kassab, a naval surgeon in World War II, continued the tradition of experimentation which marks this particular garden. One can easily see the doctor's penchant for neat knots and ties in the way in which the plants are trussed up.

Entering this garden through the hedge of Alberta spruce, one sees approximately 80 varieties of climbing roses arranged along the three sides and about 1,400 rose shrubs laid out in 3-foot beds, covered with white rose petals that serve as mulch. Scattered throughout the grounds are many specimens of unusual trees: *Auricaria*, umbrella pine, *Davidia* and dawn redwood, to mention some of the more exotic. The two specimens of Katsura date from 1887, gifts of Admiral Dewey to the first owner, Simon Gratz. Norway spruce, white oak and tulip poplar are also centennial trees.

The Kassabs have made a specialty of hollies, and the collection is particularly rich in representatives of this genus, both New World and Old. And it was in the hollies that Dr. Kassab found his "species of eternity" in a hybrid of Chinese holly, *Ilex* "Dr. Kassab." A fine specimen of Joseph Kassab's holly stands at the northeast corner of the rose garden, representing the walls and columns of a cathedral.

The heart of the Wallingford rose garden is located at the south central end of the plot, behind the solarium, nursery area and greenhouse. It is here where, in a perfumed mulch pile, spent Queen Elizabeth, Love, Peace, Don Juan and recent and legendary blooms mingle their rose remains to keep the cycle of life going.

The Wallingford rose garden was officially chartered after Dr. Kassab returned from World War II and is privately operated and family owned. The gardens are open by appointment only and admission is free.

Species and hybrids of azaleas and rhododendrons come into their full glory in naturalistic plantings

The Jenkins Arboretum

I would like it to look like the forest that William Penn found.

GEORGE PATTON, landscape architect

LOCATED IN Devon, Pennsylvania, off Berwyn-Baptist Road, the Jenkins Arboretum is a 46-acre public park dedicated to the memory of Elisabeth Phillipe Jenkins.

Elisabeth Phillipe Jenkins had a passion for animal life as well as for the garden, and in particular the birds who occupied it with her. Her invalid husband H. Lawrence Jenkins (who died in 1968), in recognition of her passion, endowed a foundation in her name to develop the garden as a "public park, arboretum and bird sanctuary." In 1971 Louisa P. Browning, owner of an adjoining 26-acre property, added her estate to the foundation.

Spring is the season of particular interest in this park, where 600 species and hybrids of azaleas and rhododendrons come into their full glory in naturalistic plantings. The design of the park is the work of prominent Philadelphia landscape architect the late George Patton, who set out to recreate Penn's Woods but seems to have caught rhododendron fever along the way. In addition to the well-represented members of the heath family, an extensive collection of day lilies adds to the summer color interest. There is also an extensively labeled collection of more than 250 species of wildflowers.

Leonard Sweetman became the first director of the Jenkins Arboretum in 1974, and spent the next twelve years of his life in transforming George Patton's plan into the public park that everyone can enjoy; his son is director today.

With help from the Commonwealth's Department of Community Affairs, the Elisabeth Phillipe Jenkins Arboretum became a part of the Tredyffrin Park System in 1974.

Leonard Sweetman, first director, who also served as head of education, publicist and head gardener, lives on at the Jenkins Arboretum

The administration building has a small classroom and is regularly used by garden clubs. In front of this building is an astronomical clock that measures the advancing seasons, constructed by Leonard Sweetman shortly before he died in 1986.

"May we have been worthy stewards is our hope." JOHN T. MORRIS, 1913

Morris Arboretum of the University of Pennsylvania

The official Arboretum of the Commonwealth of Pennsylvania

"To raise the terras or sink the Grot / in all let nature ne'er be forgot." A. POPE

THE MORRIS ARBORETUM of the University of Pennsylvania is located at the northwest corner of Philadelphia. It began in the late 19th century as the country estate of John T. and Lydia T. (his sister) Morris, offspring of one of Philadelphia's oldest and largest families. Over a period of 45 years the Morrises created on this site a personal vision of the estate garden that has, as they hoped, been extended into a living center for the study of horticulture and botany.

A university garden since 1932, the 175-acre Morris Arboretum links the collectors' imperative with the desire to assemble these collections in a meaningful and artistic way. The Arboretum is a blending of the art of the landscape garden and the intellectual fabric of a university institution. It is also the grafting of the academic missions of research, teaching and outreach services onto one of this country's most complete remaining examples of the eclectic tastes of the Victorian era as expressed in the art of the landscape garden.

Visitors gain a full appreciation of the garden by entering the Compton property off Northwestern Avenue. It is here where the Morrises began to develop their landscape garden in 1887. The Bloomfield Farm, which lies to the northwest, was acquired in 1913 and is used to support the Arboretum's research programs.

The entrance drive crosses Paper Mill Creek with a picturesque 1908 pump house, with its water wheel on the left. The water was pumped out of the creek up and over the hill to a terra cotta balustraded terrace, an echo of Italian garden design. To the right of the drive the orange-tiled roof line of Chestnut Hill

One of the richest collections of Asian species to be found in the region

Many of the finest examples of their species located outside their region of origin

College dominates the horizon. An arboreal gateway is formed by a stately swamp white oak (*Quercus bicolor*) on the right and an American beech on the left (*Fagus grandifolia*). The road makes a graceful sweep to the left at a dark grove, a mixed planting of arborvitae (*Thuja placata* cv. *atrovirens*), Sawara false cypress (*Chamaecyparis pisifera*) and Hinoki false cypress (*Chamaecyparis obtusa*). Another turn to the right through a magnificent collection of magnolias, past a rock wall of native Wissahickon stone and the George D. Widener Education Center, the original carriage house of the Morrises comes into view.

The landscape of the Morris Arboretum is a mosaic of three major landscape systems. To the north of the Widener Center, along Wissahickon Creek, are the woods, a "conserved landscape." It contains remnants of that great eastern deciduous hardwood forest which once covered the hills in this area. The "working" landscape is represented by the Bloomfield Farm. The English Park, Azalea Park, the Rivinus Rose Garden, Victorian Fernery, Love Temple, Swan Pond and other garden features make up the "symbolic" landscape, composed in the style of the 17th and 18th century English landscape garden.

The Arboretum contains one of the area's most comprehensive collections of trees and shrubs, more than 5,800 identified and labeled. John Morris corresponded with Charles Sprague Sargent, the director of Harvard's Arnold Arboretum, and through these exchanges, seeds from plant explorers in Asia, notably Ernest (Chinese) Wilson, found their way to the Morris Arboretum. As a result, the Morris Arboretum has one of the richest

Witch Hazel

The original Fernery designed by John T. Morris

collections of Asian species to be found in the region and many of the finest examples of these species located outside their region of origin. Scattered throughout all of these stately specimen trees are saplings which indicate that the enterprise of collecting did not stop with the Morrises. This is a collection that is actively curated today.

Since 1975 the Morris Arboretum has been administered as one of several Interdisciplinary Resource Centers of the University of Pennsylvania. As such, the Arboretum's professional staff are actively engaged in teaching and research programs in the biology, landscape architecture, urban and regional planning departments. Adult education courses are offered through the University's College of General Studies.

The Dorrance H. Hamilton Fernery restored and dedicated in 1994

Chapter 3

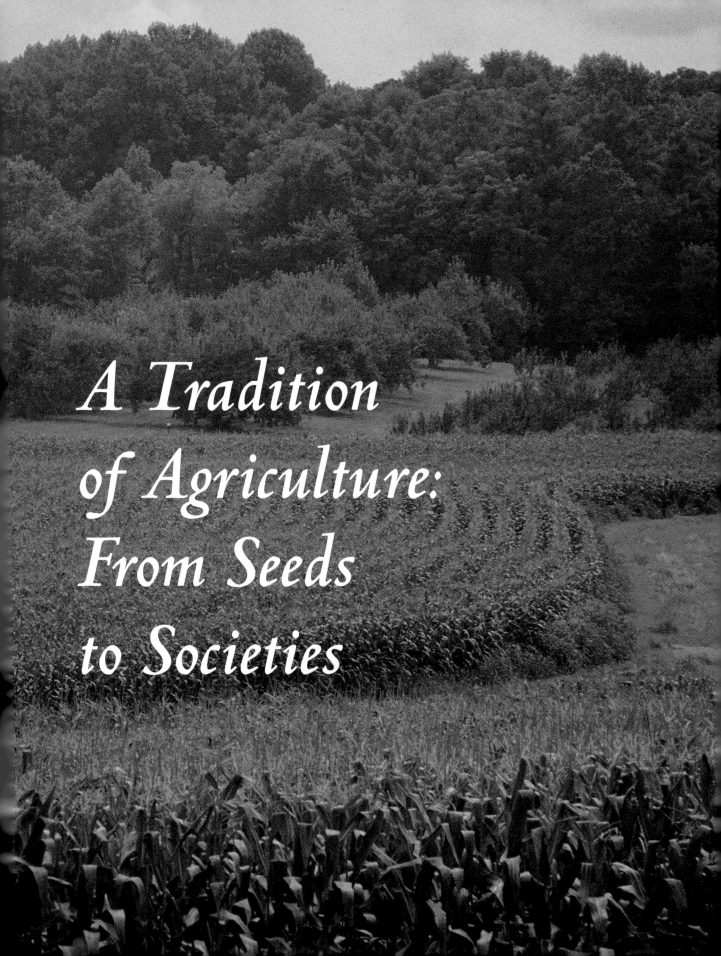

A Tradition
of Agriculture:
From Seeds
to Societies

The successful blending of garden club interests with commercial nurseries accounts for the Philadelphia Flower Show being such a large and successful enterprise

OVERLEAF: *Delaware Valley College*

*T*HE EARLY SETTLERS found an agricultural tradition more than 3,000 years old when they arrived in the Delaware Valley. Two hundred species of trees, shrubs, vines and small fruits are reported to have been in common use by the Indians, who relied heavily on corn, beans, pumpkin and squash as their chief means of sustenance. The colonists carried with them European traditions of growing plants and each wave of immigrants brought new plants and new experience in cultivation to be added to the indigenous plants and experiences that greeted them in the New World.

Before the colonists arrived, the Indians had developed the ability to force plants by hastening germination. Corn was planted in hills and there is some evidence of fertilization with fish scraps. There seems to be no evidence of crop rotation, however; the Indians of the Delaware Valley rotated their villages instead.

The Swedes first settled in Philadelphia in 1643, twenty-two years after the Pilgrims had planted their first seeds. The Dutch overthrew the Swedish authority in 1655, and the English routed the Dutch in 1664. Thus the stage was set in 1681 for King Charles II to pay a debt long owed to William Penn's father. He paid that debt with a grant of land endowed with productive soil and an agreeable climate. Here the seeds of religious freedom could be sown along with the crops to create a tradition of sharing and nurturing unrivaled by any other part of this country.

Religious persecution was the major spur to immigration. The Quaker movement with its egalitarian principles, anti-institutional views and plain country values represented the left wing of the English Reformation of the mid-17th century. Thousands of Quakers, including William Penn, were sent to prison for preaching and publishing their views. They looked to the New World for relief from persecution and they brought their gardening traditions with them.

Religious persecution forced the Germans, primarily weavers and tradespeople, out of the Palatinate beginning in 1688. Eastern European Jews immigrated two hundred years later to fill the ghettoes in the Northeast. A reform-minded rabbi from Philadelphia, Joseph Krauskopf, traveled to Russia to meet with officials and with Leo Tolstoy in search of some relief for the plight of the Jewish immigrants. With no hope of reestablishing settlements in Russia, in 1896 the Rabbi founded the non-sec-

tarian Farm School back in Philadelphia, with the objective of teaching urban youth rural values and the necessary skills to be good farmers. That school became Delaware Valley College in 1962.

The early settlers discovered what the Indians already knew: the land was highly productive and two or three men could clear twenty to thirty acres in a year. The introduction of European technology, the plow powered by horse and oxen, would transform farming from a subsistence operation into an enterprise that would create surpluses. It was also a technology that would in time transform the landscape of deep, dark woods into fields and pasturelands and eventually into landscape gardens on great estates.

Agricultural pursuits engaged most of the population, and a spirit of inquisitiveness and experimentation was abroad in the land at the highest level. Benjamin Franklin is credited with introducing rhubarb, yellow willow and kohlrabi, and Thomas Jefferson expressed his view that there can be no greater gift to an emerging nation than a useful plant.

Finding native grapes encouraged the earliest colonists to believe that they could establish a wine-making industry. The native grapes proved unsatisfactory, however, and the Swedes shifted from wild grapes and wine to planting apples and producing cider. The tangled hopes of the wine-makers can still be seen on the slopes of the Schuylkill Valley Nature Center.

Francis Daniel Pastorius experimented with grape culture after he came in 1683 as an agent of the German company and later the Frankfort Company. He purchased land from William Penn and founded Germantown, later to be settled largely by weavers and tradespeople in whose hearts dwelled a love of flowers, particularly sunflowers, hollyhocks and morning glories.

By the end of the 17th century agricultural production and gardening pursuits had become sufficiently accomplished in the colonies that Thomas Gabriel, writing in 1698, was able to comment favorably on both the quality and quantity of the produce. Many individuals contributed to this success, including Edward Shippen, a Quaker merchant, and Christopher Witt, planter of one of the first botanic gardens in this country.

William Hamilton (1745–1813) owned a property called Woodlands, in west Philadelphia, where a cemetery now stands. According to one botanical historian, William Hamilton was "the most ambitious devotee and guardian of the richest collection of native and exotic plants in America." Hamilton is also credited with introducing the Lombardy poplars and grew the Osage orange that was brought back from the Lewis and Clark expedition.

Henry Pratt, shipping merchant, brought Lemon Hill, an estate along the Schuylkill, to distinction in the 1830s. He had won prizes for his first mango, exhibited at shows sponsored by the Pennsylvania Horticultural Society, and for a "splendid specimen" of poinsettia. Lemon Hill was described as the "showplace of the city" by Andrew Jackson Downing in 1837, and tickets could be obtained to visit it from a counting house in the city. When Henry Pratt died in 1838 the catalogue listed for sale 2,700 plants of 700 different kinds. The city of Philadelphia acquired Lemon Hill in 1844 where a 52-acre reservoir was constructed, and it was on this estate in 1855 that Fairmount Park first began to take root.

The famed English botanist W. I. Hooker, director of the Royal Botanic Gardens, Kew, sent 12 seeds of *Victoria regia* to Quaker Caleb Cope. Cope's gardener was Thomas Meehan, who had been trained at Kew, and Caleb Cope had the distinction in August of 1851 of being the first to flower the Amazonian water lily in America. By the mid-19th century greenhouses were reportedly a common sight, the simple technology of the Indians forcing germination being taken to more sophisticated levels with the introduction of European glasshouse techniques. This interest in plants and their germination and dissemination was reinforced by the early development of seed houses, nurseries and an active publishing industry, all of which combined to promote the exchange of information.

By the end of the first decade of the 18th century, 400 American plants were already known in Britain. John Bartram started the first botanical garden that resembled a modern nursery, and in 1783 his son John Bartram, Jr., published a catalogue listing plants available in this nursery. In that same year, a catalogue of American plants assembled by William Young, Jr., botanist to the Queen of England, appeared in French. The competition had begun.

David Landreth, an Englishman, arrived in Philadelphia in 1781 and by 1784 had established the first seed house in this country. He was joined in the business by his sons, David and Cuthbert, and by 1824 they had devoted some 30 acres to a nursery that in 1828 was moved to Bristol. Landreth's nursery boasted some of the first stocks of camellias and rhododendrons in the city and an assortment of exotics: coral tree from South America, bananas and bird-of-paradise. In 1832 the Landreths published a 70-page catalogue listing the seeds, plants and implements that were available from their seed house.

David Landreth may have also been Bernard M'Mahon's first employer when he arrived in 1796 from Ireland. Within a few years, M'Mahon had set himself up with a seed store near Market on Second Street, and in 1806 published *The American Gardener's Calendar*, listing four thousand plants. M'Mahon had also gained the confidence of Thomas Jefferson; as a sign of this confidence he grew plants from the Lewis and Clark expedition. The influence of the great Swedish botanist and plant taxonomist, Linnaeus, is reflected in the writings of M'Mahon, who explains that the

Latin names are "for the use of such ladies and gentlemen gardeners as wish to become scientifically acquainted with the plants they cultivate."

In 1830 Robert Buist and Thomas Hibbert bought M'Mahon's nursery. Buist was an officer of the Pennsylvania Horticultural Society and wrote extensively on horticultural subjects. The rose Old Blush or Chinese Monthly, with two seasons of bloom, had been introduced from China, and selections from these introductions were propagated by Buist under the name "hybrid Perpetual Rose." In 1844 he published *The Rose Manual* that described the history and cultural requirements for 22 groups of roses. He served as the authority on the subject for many years.

An English-trained botanist from Kew, Thomas Meehan, worked as a gardener for Robert Buist and Andrew Eastwick, purchaser of the Bartram property. Meehan was corresponding secretary of the Pennsylvania Horticultural Society for years and a leader in the development of small parks throughout the city, including Bartram's Garden. In 1853 he authored the *American Handbook of Ornamental Trees*. *The Gardener's Monthly*, first issued in 1859, appeared for thirty years under Thomas Meehan's direction, pumping out information and sound advice from America's gardening capital.

The scion of another Quaker family who had arrived from England in 1683, Josia Hoopes, put together a collection of exotic plants that became the Cherry Hill Nurseries, well known in the latter part of the 19th century. *The Book of Evergreens: A Practical Treatise on the Coniferae, or Cone Bearing Plants*, was authored by Josia Hoopes in 1868. The book is a systematic survey of the conifers of the world as well as a compilation of cultural practices that the author had gained from personal experience and the writings of botanists of the period.

The tradition of seed houses and nurseries has continued in the Delaware Valley into the 20th century. In 1875 W. Atlee Burpee launched a mail order business in poultry. Subsidized rural mail delivery in the 1870s stimulated the mail order business. But Burpee switched his emphasis from poultry to seeds by the 1880s and by 1893 was claiming his firm to be the largest mail order seed house in the world. Burpee and his son David were relentless in their pursuit of excellence in their seeds, as well as ingenious promoters. They were also well ahead of their time in incorporating a research

A tradition of nurturing and sharing unrivaled by any other part of the country

arm into the company. This led to a continuing stream of new varieties. Big Boy tomatoes and marigolds are among the staples of American gardeners, and each year four million catalogues are mailed by Burpee promoting the virtues of these and new varieties.

It was only a matter of time before the increasing interest in plant gene research and the development of new varieties would coalesce into organized societies to promote the further exchange of information. The Delaware Valley has a rich assortment of the oldest and many of the strongest natural history and horticultural organizations to be found anywhere in the country.

The Philadelphia Society for Promoting Agriculture was founded in 1785. "Venerate the Plough" is the motto of this august Philadelphia society, a force in the founding of the U.S. Department of Agriculture, Pennsylvania State University and the Veterinary School of the University of Pennsylvania. The Philadelphia Society for Promoting Agriculture has its headquarters in a National Park Service building at 325 Walnut Street, the same building that the Pennsylvania Horticultural Society has called home since the 1960s.

Through Dr. John M. Fogg's interests, particularly in Magnolia, *the Morris Arboretum and Barnes Foundation still show a strong convergence in their collections*

The Academy of Natural Sciences was founded in a bakery in 1812. Now located off Logan Circle, it has one of the outstanding libraries of natural history, with many rare botanical and natural history books. The Academy is a veritable Fort Knox for natural history, a repository for the collections of flora and fauna encountered by early botanists, zoologists and ornithologists on their expeditions into the wilderness that once was the American West. Today, these collections form an invaluable resource for environmental assessment studies, as well as educating today's generations to the wonder and beauty of natural history.

By the late 19th century there was a proliferation of plant societies as interests shifted from the economic to the aesthetic, such as the Chrysanthemum Society, 1890, Carnation Society, 1891, American Fern Society, 1893, and the American Rose Society in 1899. This proliferation of societies continued well into the 20th century. In 1904 the American Peony Society was formed. Now there are societies for dahlias, orchids, delphiniums, fuchsias, cacti and three iris societies. Approximately sixty special interest plant societies are active nationally, according to a recent count, and seven of these have come into existence in the last ten years. They have a combined membership of between fifty and seventy thousand.

These interests were widely promoted by the movement to form local garden clubs. Nationally, there are approximately 15,000 garden clubs with a membership of around half a million. The Garden Club of Philadelphia was formed in 1904. Some of the most active of these clubs are counted among the 130 garden clubs of the Delaware Valley. The successful blending of these garden club interests with those of commercial nurseries by the Pennsylvania Horticultural Society accounts for the Philadelphia Flower Show being such a large and successful enterprise.

Horace Binney and James Mease were among the founding fathers of the Pennsylvania Horticultural Society in 1827 to promote the art of gardening and the pursuit of botanical science. David Landreth started the PHS Library. It is one the best in the country and still lends books out to members by mail. In 1856 the leaders of the Pennsylvania Horticultural Society were instrumental in establishing Fairmount Park. In 1866 the first Horticultural Hall was built through subscription among members.

The first flower show was held in 1829, in rooms of the American Philosophical Society. A couple of years after its founding, the first public flower show of any consequence to be held in this country was held in Philadelphia. Since then, the Philadelphia Flower Show has become the preeminent flower show in the U.S., rivaling only England's Chelsea Flower Show in popularity.

Originally, professional florists and nurserymen controled the Philadelphia Flower Show. In 1965 executive secretary (and later president) of the organization, Ernesta D. Ballard, separated the Show from the Philadelphia Flower Show Inc., and turned it into a central activity of the Pennsylvania Horticultural Society. Ernesta Ballard was a graduate of the Pennsylvania School of Horticulture for Women, which was founded by Jane Bowne Haines in 1911 to liberate women by providing careers in agriculture and horticulture. It was launched by two of the outstanding leaders in the field, Elizabeth Leighton Lee, director from 1915 to 1924, and Louise Bush-Brown, 1924–1952. It attracted a student body from all over the world, and only closed down after World War II in response to the changing role of women in society.

Since 1958 Temple University's Ambler Campus has continued the tradition of offering a blend of theoretical knowledge and practical application with a degree program in horticulture and landscape design. Co-educational since it came under Temple's administration, the open enrollment policy at Ambler has given wide access to horticulture for urban youth. For many in this region, Temple Ambler has been that needed springboard, and distinguished alumnae and alumni are making notable contributions through the Delaware Valley and beyond.

It was the impulse of the educational reformer with a passion for art that has pride of place at the Barnes Arboretum. The founder of the Barnes Foundation, Dr. Alfred C. Barnes, made his money on a successful medicine, Argerol. He had some very decided views about education and art and was closely associated with the American philosopher and educator John Dewey, who saw in education "the fundamental method of social progress and reform." Because Dr. Barnes's views, colorfully and emphatically expressed, were often at odds with the art community of Philadelphia, he was controversial and became a legend in his own time.

He established the Barnes Foundation as an art museum and art institution to remedy what he regarded as rampant visual illiteracy in Philadelphia. Art appreciation required organized study and systematic work like any other discipline, according to Barnes, and one could no more expect to gain an appreciation of art by "aimless wandering in galleries than can surgery be learned by casual visits to a hospital."

The Barnes School of Horticulture, under the guidance of Dr. Barnes's wife Laura, opened in 1940, promoting the same educational principles. It is a rigorous three-year program with two semesters each year and a course of study that balances theoretical information about plants with practical information about identification, garden design and cultural practices.

In 1945 Dr. John Fogg, Jr., a distinguished botanist and professor at the University of Pennsylvania (director of the University's Morris Arboretum from 1958 to 1968) became director of the Barnes Foundation, a position he held until 1979. Under his influence there was a movement to expand the collections botanically in support of instructional programs. An area outside the schoolhouse and office was set aside for collections of shrubs and vines. A nursery was added. Through Dr. Fogg's interest, particularly in *Magnolia*, the Morris Arboretum and the Barnes Foundation showed a strong convergence in their collections, enriching the educational experience.

When Philadelphia was founded, 90 percent of the population venerated the plow. Today, only about 5 percent of the country are engaged in agricultural pursuits. But in tracing the long history of the gardening traditions in the Delaware Valley, one finds that they have not lost their power to engage the people. Individual preoccupations around the region in the early years were brought together to form a rich mixture of societies established to promote botanical and horticultural interests. It has been this tradition of strong leadership that has made the Delaware Valley a center for the promotion of the exchange of plants and the sharing of information, creating a gateway to the gardens of this country.

Philadelphia Green—The nurturing of a gardening tradition

Reflecting "the progress of horticulture" with the planting and a respectful nod to history in the design

Pennsylvania Horticultural Society

The Heartbeat of American Horticulture

THE PENNSYLVANIA HORTICULTURAL SOCIETY is located between Third and Fourth on Walnut, next to the headquarters of Independence Park, across the way from historic Carpenters' Hall and two and a half blocks from Independence Mall. The area has been described as this country's most historic square mile. In a city which prides itself on firsts, it is a proper address for America's first horticultural society, founded in 1827.

Ten years after the founding of the Pennsylvania Horticultural Society, Andrew Jackson Downing, America's most influential landscape architect of the early 19th century, commented on the position that the Society had already attained. "It occupies a large sphere of usefulness and through means of annual exhibitions . . . disseminates knowledge of the progress of horticulture." It is at the Pennsylvania Horticultural Society where the garden lovers of this country come to feel the strongest pulse of American gardening.

Adjoining the PHS headquarters buildings are two small demonstration gardens. The Walnut Street garden has plantings arranged in divided, raised beds in the style of colonial gardens. Today the garden gives a respectful nod to the historical authenticity of that style. In the selection of varieties and the massing of color, however, this garden is designed to reflect "the progress of horticulture" rather than present a history lesson. The PHS garden designers have discovered what the French have known for centuries and before them the Romans: gardens are stages upon which the human drama must be enacted every year. This garden reflects Philadelphia's love of history but also its commitment to horticultural

The Harvest Show with an emphasis on the practical

progress, especially with regard to the challenges of planting flowers in a harsh urban environment.

But the garden at Walnut is merely the box office. The great stage for the Pennsylvania Horticultural Society is the Civic Center, where the Philadelphia Flower Show is held each year. Since its commercial beginnings in 1926, it is a show that has gotten bigger, brighter and better every year. It covers the largest indoor stage, six acres, of any flower show in the world, and over the eight-day run has an audience of almost a quarter of a million people.

Each of the Philadelphia Flower Shows represents a three-year drive from conception to staging. The themes are carefully devised to be sufficiently broad to give scope for the imagination yet provide an organizing element for exhibitors. There are 500 exhibits that explore the dimensions of these themes. But the heart of the show is the 60 major exhibits produced each year by area nurserymen, educational institutions, corporations and governmental agencies. The flower show business in Philadelphia is big business, and the major exhibitors exploit that to the hilt with ever more exciting and dramatic displays.

The Philadelphia Flower Show places a premium on what's new: new varieties, innovations in design, technological advances. The advent of refrigerated carriers and overnight

Immigrants brought new plants and new experience in cultivation to be added to the indigenous plants and experiences that greeted them in the New World

freight has made it possible to bring in flowers from the garden markets of the world. The advanced technologies of micropropagation, particularly with orchids, are already apparent in the shows. Can the products of gene splicing be far behind?

The other great show of the Pennsylvania Horticultural Society is the Harvest Show, which is held in October each year. For the past few years this show has been held in the Horticulture Center of Fairmount Park. While more modest in size, nevertheless it is widely regarded as the insider's show, the show for the initiated gardener. It is as practical as the Philadelphia Flower Show is fanciful, a celebration of the fruits of labor, with canned

goods, the biggest and best-formed cabbages, peppers, beets, in short the best that the Delaware Valley has to offer in the art and culture of plants. Judges for these shows are brought in from all over the world, the silver bowls, plates and colored ribbons fiercely contested.

But what makes the Pennsylvania Horticultural Society special is not only the production of these great shows, but the way in which the accumulated wisdom and knowledge of all these agricultural and horticultural traditions are recycled through the community. The Philadelphia Green Program, directed by the Pennsylvania Horticultural Society, traces its roots back to the early 1950s when the

Philadelphia Green traces its roots back to the early 1950s

Philadelphia Committee of the Garden Club of America organized neighborhood associations and was building pocket parks. From 1974 to 1994 Philadelphia Green had planted 2000 community gardening projects with a staff that had grown from 2 to 40. In 1993 the eighth "Greene Countrie Towne," a neighborhood where community gardening efforts are spread over a several block area, was dedicated.

Through Philadelphia Green a gardening tradition has been nurtured in the public schools, propagated through numerous community groups and borne fruit in a number of public spaces—the Philadelphia Art Museum, City Hall and waterfront areas. Trees are being planted, mini-parks established and vacant lots are sprouting green of a new edible and aesthetic kind where weeds once grew. Most important, the tradition of gardening is being propagated from one generation to another in the inner city.

The most recent annual report shows the Philadelphia Horticultural Society still providing more than 20 per cent of the support for Philadelphia Green. As the momentum for the program has gathered over the years, however, support has been widened to include a number of foundations, corporations and local, state, and federal governmental agencies. In 20 years Philadelphia Green staff have also consulted with representatives from 25 cities interested in establishing programs to green their cities.

It is a daunting job in any city, but particularly so in an old one such as Philadelphia. But the core belief of any gardener must be one of optimism; its what keeps them young at heart. And each year this growing cadre of gardeners gird themselves to face the harsh realities of life in the inner city—believing that from the inspiration of a single window box some vacant lot may come to a new flowering. And from that vacant lot may come the inspiration for an entire neighborhood to commit to the garden ethic as a way of rebuilding their communities. It is a simple, organic approach to the regreening of Penn's "Greene Country towne."

The Pennsylvania Horticultural Society is a membership organization that directs a variety of programs. On its headquarters site, there is the library with both books and catalogues of all kinds for the gardener. The society's horizons are expanded by tours, lectures and demonstrations, which attend both to the social and intellectual needs of the more than 10,000 members. The oYcial house organ, Green Scene, is a full-color magazine that keeps the membership informed of what is new and continues to point the path of horticultural progress.

Shades of the noted women who nurtured a tradition of horticulture still stalk these grounds

Temple University Ambler Campus

THE 187-ACRE Ambler campus of Temple University is located about 20 miles north of Philadelphia in Montgomery County. With 350 full-time faculty members and 5,000 students, it is the northernmost reach of an urban university that stretches along Broad Street from Center City. Within this suburban campus is Temple University's School of Horticulture and Landscape Architecture.

Entering the campus off Meetinghouse Road, one is greeted by colonial architecture and the vestiges of the 18th century farm landscape. The beginnings of this site as a teaching landscape date to 1911 and the Pennsylvania School of Horticulture for Women, founded by Jane B. Haines, Bryn Mawr class of 1891.

Some of the trees and boxwood hedges are legacies of the most prominent landscape designers of the past. Elizabeth Leighton Lee, Director of the Pennsylvania School of Horticulture for Women from 1915 to 1924, is said to have contributed designs for the campus. She was the first woman to practice landscape architecture in Pennsylvania. James Bush-Brown drew up a landscape plan for the campus and designed the gardens around some of the buildings. His greater claim to fame, however, may have been as husband of Louise Bush-Brown, director of the School from 1924 to 1952. The Olmsted brothers' firm was retained to do a survey of the campus and prepare a plan for expansion in the late 1920s. Beatrix Farrand developed a design for twin arbors. Whether the existing twin arbors are those that she designed seems doubtful, but her name and those of the other designers convey the prominent position that the Pennsylvania School of Horticulture for Women once held.

Amid the English boxwood and Japanese cherry, and beside the shaded walks, is one of this area's fine teaching collections. These specimens find their way into a variety of curriculum units, and for the visitor the collec- tion provides a valuable resource of labeled information. For those with a preference for indoor plants there are seven greenhouses that can be toured. Beyond the formal gardens are the woodlands with their delicate spring

bulbs, and beyond them, the orchards.

Today, the rationale for the school is built upon environmental issues. The crusaders from these shady groves bearing their baccalaureates will emerge to fight urban blight and pollution and to re-vegetate our parks and gardens. Where women's rights was once the unifying force, the ecological imperative is being offered up as the new theology to save the environment.

To the south of the railroad tracks are fields and orchards where peaches, cherries, apples and blueberries are grown

Delaware Valley College of Science & Agriculture, Henry Schmieder Arboretum

Lead the tens of thousands of people to your idle, fertile lands, and you will bless not only them, but also your country.

LEO TOLSTOY

THE DELAWARE VALLEY COLLEGE campus is located in Bucks County, bracketed on the East by the historic Wayside Inn, built by an Englishman in 1751, and on the West by Burpee's Fordhook Farm. The shady groves, tree-lined walks and playing fields give no hint of the singular vision which gave rise to this unique institution.

Founded as the National Farm School in 1896, the Delaware Valley College of Science and Agriculture represents another of Pennsylvania's holy experiments. It is the inspiration of one of Philadelphia's most noted reform-minded rabbis, Dr. Joseph Krauskopf (1858–1923). Rabbi Krauskopf came to the U.S. in 1872, and his vision was to create a nurturing institution that would reconcile Jews to the land while at the same time serve as an escape valve for Jewish immigrants, who since the 1880s had been fleeing Russia and crowding into cities along the northeastern seaboard.

The college controls over 750 acres of land which was originally part of William Penn's "walking purchase" of 1683, an area circumscribed by how much territory could be covered in a three-day walk. (It was purchased with wampum, blankets, kettles and beads.) The main entrance to the 45-acre campus is along a curving, chestnut oak-lined drive. English Georgian, Italian and Colonial styles of architecture can be detected on the buldings, many of which date to the period 1916–1928, when the school was undergoing rapid expansion led by President Herbert L. Allman and carried out by Philadelphia architect Lewis Magaziner.

Fine old specimen trees can be found

Fine old specimen trees can be found scattered over the campus

scattered over the campus: oak, ginkgoes lining a walk, Japanese maple, and a monumental sycamore that must trace its beginnings back to the time of William Penn. Since the early 1980s there has been a vigorous planting program, and many of the present specimens have been rescued from construction sites. The trees are carefully labeled and in recent years several new garden features have been added: rock gardens, dwarf conifers and the Hillman family garden. The whole area has been renamed the Henry Schmieder Arboretum in honor of a respected member of the college faculty.

Along the southern edge of the main campus, more than 16,000 square feet are maintained under glass. Another 6,000 feet of greenhouse are maintained at Fordhook Farm. In these growing ranges a wide variety of plants is nurtured, including cyclamens, poinsettias and bedding plants. Vignettes of new directions in horticulture are provided by student projects, and the growing facilities may be toured by appointment. To the south of the SEPTA railroad tracks are fields and orchards where peaches, cherries, apples and blueberries are grown.

The Delaware Valley College has grown from its humble beginnings as a non-sectarian farm school in 1896 through several cycles of expansion. In 1926 it became the co-educational National Agricultural College and in 1948 it was awarded full college status under its present name. Chemistry and biology were added to the curriculum in 1960 and a Business Administration major in 1964. Today, the Delaware Valley College is one of three private agricultural colleges in the United States and the nursery for many area leaders in horticulture.

OPPOSITE:
In the annual trials of the Delaware Valley College the echo of trials of other times and other places

A soothing pond with a cozy teahouse is tucked into a corner of the property

The Arboretum of the Barnes Foundation

A gallery of beautiful living specimens.

FRANK A. SCHREPFER,
landscape architect to Albert Barnes

Trees were to be grown as singular objects for their rarity and artistic merit, but they were also to be components of a larger canvas

THE WORLD-FAMOUS art collection of Dr. Albert C. Barnes (1872–1951) contains more than 1,000 paintings. What is not so well known by the community of art enthusiasts, but widely acknowledged by the horticultural and botanical communities, is that this art collection, housed in Merion, Pennsylvania, is surrounded by a distinguished collection of trees and shrubs. It is here where the visual arts and the garden arts meet.

While Albert Barnes was assembling his paintings and other *objets d'art* in the 1920s and 1930s, his wife Laura Leggett Barnes (1875–1967) was given the responsibility of developing the garden. As the visual arts were the passion of Dr. Barnes, so horticulture was the passion of his wife. From the time they were married in 1901, they would take frequent trips to Europe to indulge their passions, collecting paintings and touring the famous gardens.

Albert and Laura Barnes had a head start in the direction of building an arboretum when they purchased their 12-acre property in Merion in 1922 from Captain Joseph Lapsley Wilson. Wilson had acquired the property in the 1880s and by 1887 had assembled a respectable collection of trees and shrubs. Some of these trees go back to the Wilson era and have reached noble proportions, such as *Hovenia dulcis*. When Wilson sold the property to Dr. Barnes it was with the understanding that the trees were not to be in any way harmed by the future development.

Since 1922 a living collection of more than 1,000 accessioned plants has been assembled. A great sweep of lawn to the west of the art gallery terminates in a woodland of stately

trees. An early collection objective was to have a shady representative of each genus of conifer. The collection is also particularly rich in species of maple (*Acer*), buckeye (*Aescelus*), barberry (*Berberis*), *Magnolia* and oak (*Quercus*). An understory of *Rhododendron*, dogwood (*Cornus*), *Corylopsis* and laurel (*Kalmia*) adds to the lushness of the woodland. Laura Barnes had a particular fondness for ferns, and assembled one of the region's outstanding collections, including more than 90 species of hardy specimens. Architectural and water features were added to complete the composition. A soothing pond with cozy teahouse is tucked into a corner of the property.

The initial impulse of this collector's garden was strikingly different from any of the other gardens in the area. Plants were selected for their color, texture, seasonal change and floral display. Here Degas was to resonate

with *Davidia*, and Matisse with *Magnolia*. Beech trees and Stewartias were to be grown as singular objects for their rarity and artistic merit, but they were also to be components of a large canvas. This was Laura Barnes's living landscape, her ever-changing art gallery.

Her husband's art required a different environment. His gallery was designed by the noted architect Paul Philippe Cret, a Frenchman who had come to Philadelphia to teach at the University of Pennsylvania. Construction started in 1922. Near the gallery, formal plantings were installed with a rose garden and arbor. Specialty collections of lilac, *Viburnum*, dwarf conifers and a heath garden were later planted nearby. A collection of nearly 200 lilacs was originally selected for their color, graduating from lighter to deeper shades of purple. A remnant of this collection reminds us of a collector's garden that drew its original inspiration from visual delight and aesthetic consideration.

The Arboretum of the Barnes Foundation is privately endowed. It is overseen by a five-member board of trustees. A program of evaluating the living collections has been undertaken and a six-year cycle of pruning and fertilization regime established for the fine old specimens. A collection policy to guide the introduction of new species is also being developed as a way of arbitrating the artistic and scientific values of the collection. For unlike the art collection, whose policy and interpretive program were firmly established by Dr. Barnes, a living collection cannot be frozen in time.

OPPOSITE: *Plants were selected for their color, texture, seasonal change and floral display*

Chapter 4

The Garden as Art

Adolph Rosengarden's Chanticleer

OVERLEAF: *Doe Run Farm*

*T*HE CONQUEST of suburban spaces was accomplished by the first tentative trails and paths into the deep woods. These were followed by dirt roads, then improved roads and eventually by traction lines with horse-drawn cars. Railroads with steampowered engines first appeared in Germantown in 1830 and by the middle of the 19th century the outlying areas had been drawn to within easy commuting distance from the city. The move to the countryside gave rise to a distinctive group of gardens reflecting the passion to extend the walls of the house to encompass outdoor spaces and to convert all of nature into the art of the landscape garden.

One of the earliest estates to be developed in this fashion was Wyck, originally bought by a Quaker immigrant, Hans Millan, shortly after he arrived in Germantown in 1689. But it is from Reuben Haines (1786–1831), who married Jane Bowne in 1812, that we learn most about the garden at Wyck. Reuben had a personal interest in flower painting, was a founding member of the Academy of Natural Sciences and the Pennsylvania Horticultural Society, and a member of the Society for Promoting Agriculture. He was also a patron of the arts, including the great natural history painter, John J. Audubon.

From correspondence between Reuben and Jane Haines we gather a touching picture of their relationship and the role that the garden played in their lives. In a letter of 1817 or 1818 Jane writes to Reuben: "I hope to have honeysuckles and roses planted round the Arbour—and Lilacks, Snowballs, and double Altheas at the end of the new path—if convenient a larch tree somewhere and the Bigonia radicans by those old trees in the front yard. S. Johnson said last summer she would give me some roots of both common and variegated periwinkle. . . ."

Reuben Haines responds affectionately to his wife, "with what pleasure will I not welcome thee to the scene of my present interesting occupations, put under thy tender charge the garden and see thy taste displayed in every shrub, and in the light festoons of every vine trace the hand that gave them grace."

With convenient rail transportation in the mid-19th century the suburbs became easily accessible. The blight of the urban areas had also become sufficiently oppressive to encourage those who could afford it to flee to the outlying countryside. It was a

Reuben and Jane Haines' Wyck

Ebenezer Maxwell's Mansion

flight winged by the persistent desire to preserve that attachment to the land and powered by money to be made in land speculation. The 1859 Ebenezer Maxwell Mansion, and the houses on Walnut Lane and Tulpehocken Avenue, part of the historic district of Germantown, are prime examples of that movement.

Andrew Jackson Downing (1815–1852) became one of the leading spokesmen for the movement. The lyrical writings of this landscape designer provided the justification as well as a practical methodology for the conquest of space. Downing dared hope that he could elevate American landscape gardening to the high art it had already achieved in Britain and on the continent. But his appeal is not simply to create beautiful surroundings. Downing issued a call that is rooted in the very beginnings of Western mythology. "The love of country is inseparably connected with the love of home," Downing states in the preface of his classic, *A Treatise on the Theory and Practice of Landscape Gardening* (1841), "Whatever, therefore, leads man to assemble the comforts and elegances of life around his habitation tends to increase local attachments, and render domestic life more delightful; thus not only augmenting his own

Anabel Parson's Appleford/Parsons-Banks

The Pennock's Meadowbrook Farm

enjoyment, but strengthening his patriotism, and making him a better citizen. And there is no employment or recreation which affords to mind greater or more permanent satisfaction than that of cultivating the earth and adorning our own property."

The Picturesque style of Downing is echoed in the Gothic style architecture of Maxwell Mansion, "with bold projections, deep shadows, and irregular outlines." Its variety and irregularity of form had made it a popular style for landscape gardening in the pre-civil war era. Downing speculates that perhaps the rarity of the picturesque landscape and the contrast it provided were factors. He also suggests that its popularity may find some support in the "imperfection in our natures by which most of us sympathize more with that in which the struggle between spirit and matter is more apparent, than with that in which the union is harmonious and complete."

Frank Jessup Scott (1829–1919) takes up where Downing leaves off in a booming post-civil war economy. His widely read book on domestic beautification, *Suburban Home Grounds*, published in 1870, found a receptive audience. As with Downing, Scott searches for a philosophical basis in which to root this powerful instinct to garden. "We are not made to be content on nature's lower levels," Scott challenges us, "for that spark of divinity within us—Imagination—suggests to us progress and improvement, and these are not less natural than existence. The arts which make life beautiful are those that graft upon the wildings of nature the refinements and harmonies which the Deity through the imagination is ever suggesting to us."

Scott designs his landscapes "principally for that great class of townspeople whose daily business away from their homes is a necessity, and who appreciate more than the very rich or the poor all the hearts cheer, the refined pleasures, and the beauty that should attach to a suburban home." Never was there a more elevated description of the first commuters. In his Picturesque style, Downing is unabashedly romantic about nature. Scott, in contrast, urges his readers "not to reproduce the rudeness of Nature . . . but to adapt her to our civilized necessities, to idealize then improve, to condense and appropriate her beauties, to eliminate the dross from her vegetable jewels, and give them worthy setting—these are the aims of Decorative Gardening."

Two major themes have dominated Western gardening traditions and both are well represented in the gardens of the Delaware Valley: the garden as an extension of the house, a series of outdoor rooms with formal, rectilinear geometry; and the garden as a series of refinements of the landscape, curvilinear, informal lines extending views in a naturalistic fashion. Wyck, Maxwell, Appleford/Parsons-Banks and Meadowbrook Farm exemplify the former, and Pennypacker Mills, Chanticleer and Doe Run the latter.

The formal style traces its roots back to the very beginnings of gardening in the Western tradition, the walled Egyptian gardens of 1500 B.C. with geometric plantings of palms and fruit trees and rectangular pools teeming with fish and fowl. The terraces of the Hanging Gardens of Babylon were built between 604 and 562 B.C. Formal geometric patterns serve as the inspiration for the paradise gardens of Persia. Pliny the Younger, a Roman of the 1st century A.D., had a garden appointed with sculpture and clipped hedges, a house and garden of one integrated design. But for sheer opulence and grandeur in the formal style, there is nothing to rival Versailles, designed by Andre le Nôtre in the late 17th century for Louis XIV.

In 18th century England the formal style of gardening was rejected in favor of the

OPPOSITE: *Sir John Thouron's Doe Run*

naturalistic style. The battle lines were drawn by the literary figures of the time, and a distinguished series of garden designers occupied center stage: William Kent, Lancelot (Capability) Brown and Humphry Repton. Many of the finest formal gardens were destroyed to make way for what became known as the English style of landscape garden. The wisdom of that wholesale destruction has been called into question. The battle still rages.

The debate in garden styles moved to America in the 19th century. Downing condemns the "ancient or formal style" as being "tamed and subdued, or as some critics will have it, tortured into every shape which the ingenuity of the gardener could suggest." For his taste, trees should be disposed around the houses and parklands in all varieties of mass and small groupings, "in such a manner as to rival the most beautiful scenery of general nature."

By the latter half of the 19th century, the two styles are joined in the name of

Chanticleer

Wyck, grape arbor

Victorian eclecticism (as in the Morris Arboretum). Frank Scott diplomatically embraces all possibilities in his effort to beautify the suburban home. "No one style may say to another, 'thou art false because thou hast no prototype in nature,' since our dwellings and all the conveniences of civilized life would be equally false if judged by that standard."

Meadowbrook Farm, the masterpiece of Mr. and Mrs. J. Liddon Pennock, Jr., is the most complete example of the formal style, and also one of the most widely publicized private gardens in this country. The spatial relationships in Mr. Pennock's meticulously planned landscape have evolved over the years into a series of interconnecting indoor and outdoor rooms reflecting changing interests, new acquisitions and varying notions about how best to control the surroundings. The Parsons-Banks Arboretum, largely designed by Thomas W. Sears for Anabel Parsons, is another example of this style of garden rooms expressing different themes, aided by carefully selected plantings.

In contrast, Judge Samuel W. Pennypacker, Governor of the Commonwealth of Pennsylvania from 1903 to 1907, chose the naturalistic style for his landscape on the east bank of the Perkiomen Creek, which he bought in 1900. With a passion for American history and desire to create a family estate befitting one of his high office, farmhouse is transformed into manor house, and farmscape into the art of the landscape garden. The pastoral ideals reflected in 17th and 18th century literature are reaffirmed in Pennypacker, now preserved as a public trust.

Chanticleer, in Radnor, borrows its name from English literature, one of the fine English castles described in a novel by Thackeray, which according to the late owner shared the status of its English counterpart in that it was "mortgaged up to the window." Adolph G. Rosengarten, Jr., the second generation of the family to occupy this site, was a lawyer, businessman and military historian. He set himself the task of commanding this landscape while preserving a family tradition of gardening. One of the most intriguing aspects of Chanticleer is the way it traces the historical development of western gardens: the formal gardens to the south of the manor constructed in 1913 giving way to the naturalistic style as the gardens descend the hill. And now in the latest garden development, Chanticleer returns to its formal beginnings, as an old tennis court is replanted into a parterred garden.

When Sir John Thouron and his wife, a distant du Pont cousin, took up residence at Doe Run Farm in 1954, the present manor house was a hunting lodge. The pastures extended to the doorsteps and horses poked their heads through the windows. The landscaping consisted largely of the old orchard to the west of the entrance drive and the mature hemlock, spruce and Kentucky coffee trees that still frame the doorway. From these modest beginnings, and with inherited wealth on both sides of the family, the words of the poet Alexander Pope are brought vividly to mind, "Order in variety we see, / And where, tho' all things differ, all agree."

The entrance through the Torii Gate at Swiss Pines brings us into another world order. Here Western gardening traditions bow to the East in a microcosm of nature artfully arranged to produce a feeling of harmony and tranquillity. The formal style of the Italian and French gardens with their symmetrical arrangements and brilliant use of color make a statement of perfection achieved; in a sense, celebrations of the hu-

Swiss Pines, spring, moss, stream

man intellect over nature. The Japanese garden, no less contrived, is more a celebration of nature alone. It is a garden designed to humble but at the same time to enlighten the human spirit. The Japanese preference for implied rather than explicit modes of communication envelop the visitor. By its design we are invited to participate, to apply the imagination to a particular scene, to add the missing elements implied by odd-numbered parts and asymmetrical arrangements, or to be reminded of a place in nature that has some special meaning.

The development of this area of Charlestown started with a deed from William Penn to Charles Pickering. By 1895 the property was owned by Llewelyn Welsh, who used it as a summer residence. Like so many of his contemporaries, Mr. Welsh was an ardent traveler and collector, and numbered among his collections were three Japanese lanterns. The spoils of his travels, as in other collectors' gardens, find a place on the grounds of his summer home. The wheel turns, and these reminders of distant places are eventually to provide the inspiration for what comes after.

Perhaps Arnold Bartschi and his wife, Meta, immigrants from Switzerland in 1920, heard the distant echo of their homeland from one or more of the forty-two Swiss stone pines planted on the property. The Japanese lanterns illuminated the next phase of development. Between 1966 and 1969 Mr. Bartschi retained the respected garden designer, Katsuo Saito, to consult on the design of an authentic Japanese Garden to be created at Swiss Pines. Mr. Bartschi next employed Hiroshi Makita, a student of Zen Buddhism and an immigrant to this country from Japan in 1970, and one who was later to distinguish himself as a garden designer of considerable talent in his own right. Makita worked at Swiss Pines from 1970 to 1981, helping bring the Japanese garden to fruition.

Thus the lanterns, once appearing in the landscape as trophies from a late Victorian traveler, at last find a home in a Japanese garden in Chester County, Pennsylvania, surprisingly enough in a place called Swiss Pines. And for more than thirty years, Arnold Bartschi pours his imagination, labor and financial resources into this garden treasure. It is a garden where truly East meets West, and as in the real world, the meeting sets into motion new harmonies and old dissonances.

In the relentless quest to surround ourselves with spaces we can take pleasure in, these nine gardens represent the major trends that have taken place over a period of 300 years. We can see in them the struggle to find artistic expression and also to assert artistic ownership. They also tell us something about our changing attitude toward nature and our place in it.

OPPOSITE: *Arnold Bartschi's Swiss Pines*

"See thy taste displayed in every shrub, and in the light festoons of every vine trace the hand that gave them grace."

REUBEN TO JANE HAINES

Wyck

With what additional pleasure will I not aid thee imparting instruction to our daughter and after the daily task has been cheerfully peformed lead her forth into the garden. . . .

Reuben Haines *to* Jane B. Haines, 1818

The BAILIWICK of nine generations of Quaker Philadelphians, Wyck is located at 6026 Germantown Avenue, six miles north of Center City, at the corner of Walnut Lane. It is the intersection of innovative expressions of architecture represented in the 1824 work of William Strickland, designer of the Second Bank of Philadelphia.

The site has been gardened since the late 17th century, when Wyck emerged as a clearing in the wilderness. Over the years it has been transformed by the growing wealth of generations of Haineses, who extended the noble architecture into garden rooms, creating on this two and one half acre site one of Philadelphia's most historic houses and gardens.

The parterred plan of this garden is from Jane B. Haines's "Plan of Garden" 1821–1827. An arbor was added in 1814, and by 1827 Jane was growing about two dozen varieties of roses. Wyck is still one of the best places in the city to find old-fashioned roses, which reach their peak of flowering in June.

During the long tenure of Jane Reuben Haines (1832–1911), the unmarried daughter of Reuben and Jane, Wyck had the look of one of those lush, overgrown Victorian gardens. After the property was left to her nephew and niece, Caspar Wistar Haines (1853–1935) and Jane Bowne Haines (1869–1937, founder of the Pennsylvania School of Horticulture for Women), some of the luxurance of the Victorian era was trimmed back to the more disciplined Colonial Revival look. It was during this time that the first steps were taken to place Wyck in public trust. The transfer from

"I hope to have honeysuckles and roses planted round the arbor."   Jane to Reuben Haines

private to public purpose was completed during the ninth generation of Haineses, nurseryman Robert Bowne Haines of New Jersey and his wife Mary.

Wyck is on the National Register of Historic Sites and under consideration as a National Historic Landmark. Since 1937, it has been maintained by the Wyck Charitable Trust and the Wyck Assocation. By the mid-1980s, Wyck had evolved into a complete historic property, housing over 100,000 documents and other family papers.

"*The arts which make life beautiful are those that graft upon the wildings of nature the refinements and harmonies which the Deity through the imagination is ever suggesting to us.*"   FRANK J. SCOTT

Ebenezer Maxwell Mansion

The architecture which belongs to the

picturesque landscape is the Gothic mansion,

the Old English or Swiss Cottage,

or some other striking forms. . . .

ANDREW JACKSON DOWNING, 1859

THE EBENEZER MAXWELL MANSION is located in the Germantown section of Philadelphia at the intersection of Tulpehocken and Greene Streets, six miles from the center of the city. A visit to Wyck or Ebenezer Maxwell Mansion would not be complete without a drive up Walnut Lane and Tulpehocken Avenue to view the Gothic, Queen Anne, Tudor, Georgian and Colonial Revival architecture which is so abundantly represented and has helped define this neighborhood.

Ebenezer Maxwell built his 1859 Norman Gothic-style mansion as a speculation home. Speculations in real estate were a common practice in this neighborhood in the 1850s. The idea of suburbia was still bright and shiny and the bullish market of this period catalyzed many such financial ventures. Ebenezer moved into his home (or "villa" as it was called in those days) in 1859 with his wife Anna and five children. By 1862, however, he had sold this house and moved to another that he built next door.

There are no records of what the grounds around the Maxwell Mansion looked like, and in the absence of any historic plan the restoration of Maxwell adopted the styles of landscape gardening of two of America's foremost practitioners of the art, Andrew Jackson Downing (1815–1852) and Frank J. Scott (1828–1919).

The landscape style of Andrew Jackson Downing with its variegated colors and form is presented across the front of the mansion along Tulpehocken Avenue. The period of the recreation is pre-civil war, from 1840 to 1860. Each tree and shrub grows out of a specific reference in Downing's classic work, *A Treatise*

The Frank J. Scott landscape style extends along the Greene Street side and to the rear of the mansion. It is post-civil war in conception, 1860–1880, the living documentation of one of Scott's designs published in his widely read *The Art of Beautifying Suburban Homes*, published in 1870.

According to Scott's principles, the greatest length should be devoted to an unbroken stretch of lawn. The leveled terrace provides a formal platform for the mansion and is a design taken directly out of Scott's book. Plantings radiate in lines to channel views out of the window to the cast-iron seat in front of an island of evergreens, the weeping dogwood (a favorite form for a Scott landscape), the colorful bed of annuals backed up by fruit trees and

on the Theory and Practice of Landscape Gardening, first published in 1841.

Downing describes two distinctive styles, the Picturesque and the Beautiful. The Picturesque is characterized by irregular growth, bold character, variety, thickets embellished with rustic ornaments. The pool and natural rock work, the berm in the lawn and the woods area, the singular form of the Atlantic cedar (*Cedrus Atlantica*) and weeping spruce (*Picea abies pendula*) are all elements of Downing's Picturesque landscape. The Beautiful reflects order, neatness, flowing lines and harmonious accessories. The curving drive fits perhaps best Downing's description of the Beautiful, but even here he allows the mixture of the two styles.

L. Engle, a professional landscape architect of Philadelphia, who integrated the Downing and Scott landscape styles to achieve the unity of composition that Downing would have appreciated. It was Charlotte C. Stokes, however, chair of the Maxwell Mansion garden committee, who was the driving force in this garden recreation, and author of its history, *Documentation of the Victorian Gardens at the Maxwell Mansion*. The restoration plans were approved in 1977 and the Pennsylvania Horticultural Society provided some of the first funding to begin construction. The gardens were completed in 1979. The Maxwell Mansion is a non-profit organization and in 1974 was entered on the National Register of Historic Places.

Thuja occidentalis cv. *nigra*. The foundation plantings along the bay window of *Syringa x persica* and *Deutzia gracilis* and the Hemlock gateway to the rear of the mansion are other images directly out of Scott's pattern book. Through topiary, people of modest incomes could achieve architectural elements in their landcape for maximum effect and moderate cost.

Thus in the Maxwell landscape there is a blending of two landscape styles. Both take off from the same point of departure, the house, but then diverge to reflect differing attitudes about nature: the one consciously borrowing from nature, the other looking more inward to the human creative spirit.

The mansion was twice saved from the wrecker's ball in the 1950s and 1960s. The garden was recreated under the guidance of Reed

The pond with small island was constructed in the early 1930s to the plans of the well-known Philadelphia architect, Thomas W. Sears

Appleford/Parsons-Banks

"A pleasant garden spot
for every mood and season."

ANABEL PARSONS

IN PHILADELPHIA'S western suburbs of Villanova, modest signs direct the visitor to Appleford, an elegant house surrounded by a series of garden rooms surrounded by woodland preserve and bird sanctuary. This 22-acre property belongs to Lower Merion Township and carries the official name, Parsons-Banks Arboretum.

The entrance is located at 770 Mt. Moro Road, off Spring Mill Road. White Pines line the drive, replacing the apple trees that gave the estate its name when Mr. and Mrs. Lewis Parsons lived here. The drive curves gently to the left through naturalized woodland, across a ford upgraded to bridge, bracketed by a recent planting of the Kousa dogwood (*Cornus kousa*) and ending in a public parking lot.

The Parsons-Banks Arboretum traces its ownership back to a William Penn land grant to James Moore in 1682. The stone farmhouse and other outbuildings date from the early to the late 18th century. The farmhouse was remodeled according to the design of the prominent Philadelphia architect, Richardson Brognard Okie, after the property was purchased by the Parsons family in 1926.

The pond with small island was constructed in the early 1930s to the plans of the well-known Philadelphia landscape architect, Thomas W. Sears. His design reveals the handiwork of a true plantsman, with native and introduced trees, shrubs and perennials: golden willow (*Salix vitellina*), winterberry (*Ilex verticillata*), highbush blueberry (*Vaccinium corymbosum*), Joe Pye weed (*Eupatorium purpureum*), water iris (*Iris versicolor*) and blue lobelia (*Lobelia syphillitica*). The perennial garden designed by Sears (blueprint dated

August 26, 1929), was to have been anchored at the corners by three species of shrubs and to incorporate seven kinds of vines; it lists sixty-five species of perennials.

The main garden interest at Appleford is invested in the series of garden rooms, developed in the late 1920s and 1930s. The Rose and Water Garden is planted with hybrid tea and rambler roses. The Parterre Garden to the north of the house forms an interesting pattern from the second floor, and each cell is planted with standard *Cotoneaster*. A few years ago a single Fairy rose was grown as a standard in each of these diminutive rooms, framed by clipped Box. The Walled Garden is planted as a Spring white garden.

While the garden rooms are based upon Sears's designs, they were planted under the watchful eye and active participation of Anabel Parsons (1883–1973), a prominent Philadelphian, whose portrait hangs in the living room. Her presence can still be felt on the ter-

race, one of her favorite garden rooms, where she would frequently take tea with friends and look across the wall to the pond whose course she altered to suit her tastes.

Mrs. Parsons left Appleford, along with a small endowment, to Lower Merion Township, renaming the estate the Parsons-Banks Arboretum in memory of her husband, Lewis Parsons, and Clayton Banks, her son by her first marriage, both of whom predeceased her. The garden has retained its formal character but lost much of the richness of the plantings proposed by Sears, a not unusual course of events when direction changes from private passion to public purpose. The Arboretum is managed by the Appleford Committee of Volunteers, and is a popular place for weddings, receptions and parties.

"The well designed garden to do for our mode of living much what the interior design of our house contributes to our special way of life."   J. Liddon Pennock

Meadowbrook Farm

We plant for every effect, for the seasons, for continuing flowering, for the evergreen quality, even for the bare look.

J. LIDDON PENNOCK

MEADOWBROOK FARM is located in the Huntingdon Valley suburb of northwest Philadelphia. The formal gardens are to the back of the residence, covering an area of a couple of acres of the 25-acre property. It is a garden that has been planned, planted and sculpted into existence over fifty years by the present owners, Mr. and Mrs. J. Liddon Pennock, Jr., two of Philadelphia's most distinguished citizens. Described as "one of the finest gardens in the world," Meadowbrook Farm, through its eleven outdoor rooms, demonstrates that the drive for perfection in the garden arts is alive and well in Philadelphia.

Entering Meadowbrook Farm off Washington Lane, the long curving driveway bends to the left with the nursery and extensive working greenhouses on the right. To tempt the visitor, the sales greenhouse is strategically located near the entrance. The driveway ends in a courtyard with cobblestone lines radiating from the central fountain. The spare plantings around the native stone house reflect Mr. Pennock's dislike of foundation planting, which all too often gets out of control.

The proper entrance to this garden is through the house, which was constructed in 1937 as a gift to the newlyweds from Mrs. Herkness, Alice Pennock's mother. The living room changes from winter to summer; pictures, draperies and even the sconces are rotated according to the season. All the rooms in the house are alive with flowers, producing a resonance between the interior and exterior space. This is exemplified most dramatically in the conservatory, constructed in the 1960s. Mr. Pennock describes it as the "tie that binds

pushed back the vine-covered woodland to create a remarkable series of rooms: Round Garden in the '30s and '40s, Herb Garden and swimming pool in the '50s and the Glass House and gazeboes in the '60s. (Several of the gazeboes have premiered at the Philadelphia Flower Show before being recycled at Meadowbrook Farm.) But as every gardener knows, the garden is never completed, and even though to the visitor the composition seems impeccable, Mr. Pennock, with pruning shears in his back pocket, stalks the garden in search of a plant or a branch out of place. "Good grooming," he says, "is a prerequisite to successful gardening."

Meadowbrook Farm is a private garden, open for group tours by appontment. If the group is lucky, the artist and sculptor of this elegant landscape, J. Liddon Pennock, will personally escort the tour.

house and terrace to the garden beyond." Here hanging ferns and begonias form the core of the design while *Ficus* camouflage the hardware and primroses color the white marble floors.

Stepping onto the terrace we enter the first garden room. A magnificent magnolia (*Magnolia grandiflora*) is espaliered against the south wall. Every space here is taken up with a plant, a topiary or a flower, all artfully arranged. To the south of the terrace is the circular Eagle Garden, and to the east and west we look up and down a chain of circular and rectangular gardens centered on pools, embellished with architectural features, connected by paths or stone steps, and all integrated into a variegated tapestry of plants that play their roles throughout the seasons.

There are eleven gardens, counting the conservatory, that have evolved over the years. The Pennocks started at their terrace and

"I draw and plot to scale . . . because I believe the structure of a garden should repeat the structure of the house."
J. LIDDON PENNOCK

The meadow, filled with wildflowers and tall grass, provides the perfect setting for the manor house

Pennypacker Mills

Another man writes me he has sent three chestnut trees and one extra pecan tree to Pennypacker's Mills. Put the pecan somewhere on the lawn and give it special attention. The others can go down by the stream.

Letter from JUDGE SAMUEL W. PENNYPACKER, 1904

Monarch

PENNYPACKER MILLS is located at the confluence of the Perkiomen and East Branch creeks near the base of Spring Mountain. Occupancy of this site can be traced back to the Lenni Lenape Indians who lived in this region. George Washington's troops occupied the site in the fall of 1777 after their defeat at the Battle of Brandywine and before they reengaged the British forces at the Battle of Germantown.

The entrance to the 125-acre estate is off Haldeman Road, running in a northward direction along the east side of the property. Streams and woodland along Perkiomen Creek reveal dramatic vistas of the manor house across the meadow to the east. Turning sharply to the east the drive bends toward the dark grove of evergreens anchoring the house to the west.

The meadow, filled with wildflowers and tall grass, provides the perfect setting for the house. The carefully-sited groves of oak and beech frame vistas and give scale to the setting. Clearly the hand of a master landscape designer was at work here. His name was J. Franklin Meehan, son of Thomas Meehan.

Meehan's reputation for landscapes of distinction and his Germantown nursery, which featured native trees and shrubs, suited the tastes of Governor Samuel W. Pennypacker, who presided over the building of the capitol in Harrisburg. In 1901 Meehan embarked on landscaping plans with tree and shrub inventories, but Judge Pennypacker also had strong views about plants and plant design. Not always satisfied with Meehan's work, in 1906 he dismissed him.

Swallowtail

Fritillary

Meehan's south entrance to the manor house through a grove of trees was never built, although the proposed alignment is cut through the meadow and well worth the walk to see what might have been. Near the manor house the coarse texture of the meadow gives way to more finely-maintained lawns. A mixture of native and exotic trees and flowering shrubs embellishes the grounds to distinguish this from the farmyard of the 18th and 19th centuries. The architect Arthur Brockie was retained to remodel the farmhouse, which he did in the Colonial Revival style, setting off the Picturesque style of landscape gardening that Meehan was advancing.

Over the long period of occupancy of this site, including two distantly related branches of the Pennypacker family, one can see as at few other places the evolution of the rural landscape as patterns of use changed down through the centuries, from its Indian heritage, the mill, the plantation, down to the family home and historic site of today.

The property was purchased by Montgomery County from the estate of Margaret Haussman Pennypacker in 1981, and in 1985 it was opened to the public as an historic house museum. Of the original 125 acres only about 15 acres around the manor house are maintained as a part of the historic landscape garden. The remainder of the property is leased and farmed.

OPPOSITE: *A porch for viewing butterflies on a summer afternoon*

Chanticleer traces the history of western garden development from the formal to the naturalistic

Chanticleer

*Two landscaping styles meet
in a country gentleman's garden.*

Chanticleer

LOCATED IN THE suburb of Radnor, Chanticleer is bounded on the north and west by Brooke Road and on the south by Church Road. The main entrance to the manor, at 800 Church Road, diverges at a right angle before curving sharply to the left, to arrive at the courtyard where the espaliered dwarf apple, *Enkianthus*, flowering quince and English yew mark this as a place of varied horticultural interest.

Minder House, situated northwest of Chanticleer and about 250 feet downslope, was built in 1924 and acquired in 1933. It was the residence of Adolph G. Rosengarten, Jr., whose interest in plants was first sparked by his parents when growing up in neighboring Chanticleer. The family grew a Victory Garden (of World War I) in the area of the lawned terrace and swimming pool added after the war. Chanticleer also had extensive flower and vegetable gardens.

The garden style clearly changes in the descent from the formal parterred gardens of the stucco, Norman-style architecture of Chanticleer to the more informal native-stone-built Minder House. It is the landscape around Minder House and extending out to the north and west that most clearly expresses the horticultural development of the second generation Rosengarten. Together they recapitulate the history of Western garden development, a march from the formal style of Italian and French gardening to the naturalistic English style that we associate in this country with Andrew Jackson Downing and Frederick Law Olmsted.

A series of garden rooms were developed to the south of Chanticleer: terrace, sunken

garden, grass court and swimming pool. The architectural elements for this area, balustrades, fountains, paths and tea house, were installed in the early 1930s, although the plantings continue to evolve, with, for example, ground covers and shrubbery, of which there is a fine collection artfully arranged.

In 1958 Minder House was enlarged with a morning room, flower room and library, under the supervision of Charles Willing, who also helped the family plan the gardens. A series of curving low stone walls started in 1960 and completed eight years later embrace fountains, sculpture and a sundial. They are planted at the upper end with mountain laurel (*Kalmia latifolia*), *Pieris Japonica* and *Leucothoe*, and at the lower end with roses. These architectural elements and plantings direct the view down the slope to the three-tiered stone wall, pond and woodlands beyond. The wall

was developed in the '70s because, as Mr. Rosengarten stated, "the bank could be maintained only at the risk of life and limb." The pond and surrounding area have been developed into a meadow garden.

Visually the water flows naturally from the rock garden along the spring head above it, although the pond is actually fed by Bell's Run, the brook that traverses the northern boundary of the property. Bell's Run is planted with trillium, mertensia and daffodils, forming a colorful display in the spring. The bridges, stone walls and a working overshot waterwheel that pumps water up to the gardens around the manor house, make this section with its several vistas a particularly fine example of the Picturesque style of landscape gardening.

The picturesque style of landscape gardening

Although additions to the garden, such as woodlands along Brook Road and a wildflower garden along Church Road, retain this English look, it is significant that the most recent garden development has been a return to the formal style. An old tennis court on an adjoining property has been redesigned as a parterred garden, the four quadrants planted with a mix of perennials. Thus Chanticleer returns to its roots.

Chanticleer is privately owned and operated, although it is on the National Register of Historic Places. A Chanticleer trust has been established to assure the preservation of this property and the lifestyle it represents well into the future.

Sharing the proud tradition of landscape gardening as a fine art

Doe Run Farm

I wanted to produce something to enjoy that would also teach.

SIR JOHN THOURON

AMONG THE GENTLE slopes of the Brandywine countryside is Doe Run, where the British roots of plantsman Sir John Thouron are displayed in a uniquely American landscape.

The approach through this pastoral landscape, sprouting prosperous barns and field-stone houses, gives no sign of having crossed some cultural divide. The turn onto Thouron Road, with the extensive range of greenhouses, however, begins to mark this as a special place. How special it is becomes abundantly clear at the entrance drive, lined with beech and Katsura trees. The stable, with sweet bay magnolia (*Magnolia virginiana*) espaliered against the south wall and framed by a low stone wall decorated with luxuriant perennials, foretells of wonders to come.

The gardens of Doe Run cover an expanse of about 20 acres, in an estate of around 500 acres. The double perennial border to the west of the manor is here because Sir John Thouron (son of an American father and Scots mother) grew up with perennials. A tall hemlock hedge frames a diverse array of color, form and texture, including the pink of the *Oenothera* "Rosea Mexicana," the red foliage of the *Rosa rubrifolia*, the gray-green, broadly-cleft leaves of the artichoke and the fern-leaved verbena. Sir John got the yellow iris in Scotland. "It blooms three times . . . and I've got it in yellow, white and blue." A hybrid verbena scrambling over the edge of the walk is a product of his own efforts to add to the diversity of plant life.

The Long Border to the south of the manor arcs gently around Sir John's favorite tree, a full canopied Beech (*Fagus rotundifolia*). The mounds of white phlox (*Phlox drummondii*), spikes of yellow verbascum, clary sage (*Salvia sclarea*), originating from the Vatican garden. and the pink (*Dianthus* "Rachael"), developed at Doe Run, combine to give a sense of studied casualness. A line of hemlock and spruce to the back visually connects this island with the wooded hillside beyond.

This style of island planting is one that has been popularized by another highly-regarded perennial plantsman, Alan Bloom, and it should come as no surprise that Sir John maintains an active exchange of plants with the Blooms of Bressingham. Sir John also maintains that his island beds are original with him, a bit of convergent evolution perhaps.

At the north end of the Long Border is a gathering of thirteen willows (*Salix alba* "Chermesina"). They are radically pruned (pollarded) each January to sprout a tuft of new growth that turns a brilliant scarlet in the winter. The willows came from Sir Eric Savill's garden in Windsor Great Park.

An Alpine garden that could be considered the distant cousin of the great rock garden at the Edinburgh Botanic Garden was started with stones gathered from surrounding woods and water that is gravity-fed across the fields. It is planted with a lush combination of hostas, *Astilbe* and ferns, giving way downstream to a scattering of primulas (*Primula japonica*), *Phlox*, and such rarities as *Laurentia minuta*, *Dianthus alpinus*, *Lewisia*, *Armeria maritima* and *Allium sibthorpianum*. This water and rock sculpture is set against a tapestry of spruce and rhododendron.

To the south of the Alpine Garden is a newly planted, parterred rose garden. A worm fence with Egyptian Lablab (*Dolichos Lablab*)

scrambling up in the places where the worm turns, divides cultured from uncultured landscape. The paths are paved with a distinctive mix of pink and black pebbles, found after a painstaking search by the owner.

Where horses once grazed in the pasture, the human eye now feasts on a combination of red and white poppies (*Papaver rhoeas*), blue cornflowers (*Centaurea cyanus*) and pink campions in a luscious meadow garden.

A fan stairway, designed by Sir John when a young man, leads to the terrace of the manor. With the help of his head gardener and fellow-countryman, Jock Christie, he discovered the combination of plants that would thrive in the irregular plant pockets formed on either side: *Penstemon* from the Sierras and Cascades, and a *Campanula* from South Africa, negotiated from Lady Serena James of Yorkshire.

The bed along the entrance drive in front of the stable is a mix of shrubby cinquefoil (*Potentilla fruticosa*), *Hypericum*, *Alonsoa linearis* and small yellow poppies (*Hunnemania* "Sunlite"). The kidney-shaped bed is pinned on either side by a spruce and *mugo* pine, interspersed with perennials, Russian sage, *Clematis*, hardy geraniums, yarrow, astilbes and cardinal flower (*Lobelia cardinalis*). Cultivars of the cardinal flower have been developed through Sir John's own experimental efforts at hybridization. Contained within a dry stone wall are dry bed Crocosmia "His Majesty," *Malva alcea fastigeata* and *Anemone japonica*.

Doe Run Farm is a private estate, open to gardening groups upon request, guided by Sir John himself.

OPPOSITE:
The perennial border, an invitation to nature's beauties to join in the grand pastime of converting landscape into art

A celebration of nature designed to humble and enlighten the human spirit

Swiss Pines

Where East meets West

SITUATED ABOUT halfway between Malvern and Phoenixville off Charlestown Road, this is one of the truly unique gardens of the Delaware Valley. While Swiss Pines was designed and constructed in the artistic tradition of the Japanese strolling gardens, reflecting the Japanese love of nature, a reverence for age and a preference for asymmetric arrangements in muted colors, recognition is also given to Western traditions within the garden.

The paths in this strolling garden conduct one through a series of abstract experiences from nature rather than garden rooms projecting a manor house into the landscape. Stones are carefully selected and placed throughout to give a sense of stability as well as for their symbolic meaning. In the dry garden (Karesansui) the raked pebbles may symbolize water with waves breaking along the shores of mythic islands represented by the large stones. Reminiscent of the famous Ryoan-ji in Kyoto, the dry garden of Swiss Pines was designed by the master garden designer, Katsuo Saito.

East joins West in the selection of plants, while the placement and cultural practices are strictly in the oriental tradition. The West is represented in hemlocks, hollies and yews, the East in *Cryptomeria*, maples, katsura, bamboos, azaleas and aucubas. The combination gives variety and texture to reflect the Japanese taste for more monochromatic shades of green. While the use of color is restrained, it appears in delightful ways to highlight season change: flowering cherries, the brilliant fall color of the Japanese maples and elegant irises strategically placed around pools. The ferns and mosses, featured in such gardens as Saiho-ji, appear in shady spots and most banks to

Where East meets West in a microcosm of nature artfully arranged to produce a feeling of harmony and tranquility

add their color and texture to the richness of this garden.

Water is designed to be appreciated in such subtle forms as wetness on a boulder, dew on a mossy bank, a trickle through a bamboo pipe splashing into a stone basin, sparkling down a waterfall, or even to reflect the cosmic order of things in a small pond animated by the Japanese Koi carp.

The path over arching bridges, through bamboo groves and covered walkways, eventually arrives at a beautiful and authentic tea house. Another of Katsuo Saito's designs, it is a copy of Chosho-Tei, one of the oldest of the Japanese tea houses. It is here a Zen master would conduct the tea ceremony, a communion with nature that is at the very heart of the Japanese culture.

Stone lanterns, one more than 600 years old, are sited throughout the garden. Trademarks of Japanese design, they punctuate

views as well as serving as monuments and memorials. The stone Buddha also sits in his place of honor to mark the Japanese garden's connection with religious traditions.

The path up the azalea-lined hillside leads to a 1780 pumphouse, a barn constructed in 1821 and the manor house, part of which were built in 1823. A series of Western-style gardens, including an extensive herb garden, an allee of dawn redwoods and a Pinetum, have been developed in this area and stand in marked contrast to the Japanese garden below.

The inspiration behind this garden belongs to Arnold Bartschi, a Swiss immigrant in 1920, who made his fortune making shoes. His love of nature and financial resources were stitched together to create this distinctive landscape. During the time he has lived in this area, as well as opening the garden to the public, he has deeded 250 acres of property to be maintained as preserves for educational purposes.

Chapter 5

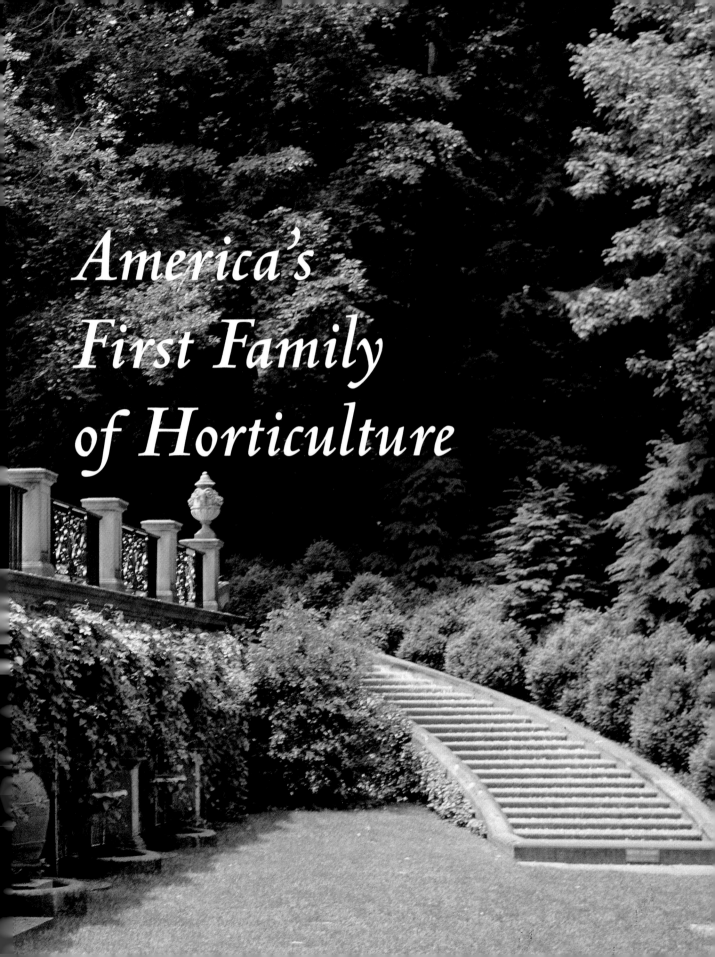

*America's
First Family
of Horticulture*

Crowninshield garden at Eleutherian Mills—an imaginative leap to transform a powder mill into a romantic, Italianate ruin garden

OVERLEAF: *Longwood Gardens*

*T*HROUGH THEIR historical development and varying styles, the six du Pont gardens of the Brandywine reveal the underlying themes of this guide: gardens as personal statements transformed from spaces maintained by necessity into artistic compositions for pleasure and finally into nature preserves.

Eleuthère Irénée du Pont (1771–1834), founder of the Du Pont Company, came to this country with his father, Pierre Samuel, wife Sophie and their three children on the *American Eagle*. They left France in October 1799 and landed at Bergen Point, New Jersey, in January 1800. Irénée's older brother Victor, a member of the French consular service in Philadelphia for eight years, eased the transition into their adopted country.

The family patriarch, Pierre Samuel du Pont de Nemours (1739–1817), was a prominent official who had served as Inspector General under Louis XVI. As a member of the physiocrats (a group of radical French economic thinkers), he had written on agricultural subjects and expounded the group's belief that all true wealth comes from the land, as opposed to the mercantilist view of wealth originating from manufacture and trade. He was a man with considerable accomplishments to his credit and with connections in high places. Thomas Jefferson asked him to advise on the establishment of an educational system for America. He also carried the message to the French court of Jefferson's desire to bring the Louisiana territory under the American flag.

The du Ponts were leaving their beloved Bois des Fosses (Forest of the Moats) located south of Paris near Nemours, acquired by the family in 1774. It was not an easy decision to make, but the constitutional monarchy that Pierre Samuel du Pont espoused was not a popular idea with Napoleon. They made a family decision to "transplant" themselves somewhere in the American frontier and establish a "rural society, Pontiana."

Although the du Ponts hoped to make their fortune in agricultural pursuits, that plan was quickly deflected by the cost of land and by friends and advisers who pointed out the need for a black powder manufacturing company in America. Encouraged by government and military officials, in the fall of 1800 the du Ponts decided to build a gunpowder factory. Charles Talleyrand (1754–1838), Napoleon's able foreign minister, arranged for Irénée du Pont to see the newest techniques of the powder industry in Paris and provided mechanical designs and machinery at cost. Talleyrand's motives were to promote the French connection in America and thwart a British monopoly on gunpowder.

In 1802 Irénée du Pont purchased from Jacob Broom 65 acres of land on the Brandywine, and his new home, Eleutherian Mills, designed by Peter Bauduy, was finished in 1803. By 1804 the first black powder was shipped out of the du Pont plant. By 1811 the Du Pont Company was well on its way to becoming the largest gunpowder factory in America.

Before leaving France, however, Irénée du Pont had clearly expressed other career intentions. On his passport he listed his profession as "Botaniste." Botany may well have been his first love, one he had inherited from his father and one that he would certainly pass on to his children. He had prepared by attending a few lectures at the Jardin des Plantes in Paris, and soon after he arrived in America he began his acquaintance with the flora of his adopted country. Later he launched a campaign to preserve the two French gardens in America established by Andre Michaux: the Jardins de la République near Bergen Point, New Jersey, and Goose Neck near Charleston, South Carolina. He wrote letters to Madame Bonaparte urging the introduction of a new variety of trees. Some of the extensive Black Oak plantings in France today may even be traced to Irénée du Pont's efforts as a collector.

Trees were also a factor in locating a powder mill on the Brandywine. Willows grew here that were needed for charcoal production in the manufacture of black powder. Thus Irénée du Pont's botanical interests and gunpowder manufacture fused on the Brandywine and changed the course of history. Eleutherian Mills became a way station for itinerant botanists at the same time it became the epicenter for an emerging black powder industry. For his efforts, Irénée du Pont was inducted into the prestigious American Philosophical Society in 1801 and the Philadelphia Society for Promoting Agriculture in 1808.

For his private garden, Mr. du Pont chose the style with which he was most familiar: parterres and trellises to contain his vegetables, vines and fruiting trees. It was a

OPPOSITE: *For his private garden, E. I. du Pont chose the style he was most familiar with: parterres and trellises to contain his vegetables, vines and fruiting trees*

utilitarian garden, but even though modest in size, it conveyed a true plantsman's interest. Three generations later, the Crowninshield Garden at Eleutherian Mills would represent an imaginative leap to transform a powder mill into a romantic, Italianate ruin garden.

Later du Pont gardens would also look to French gardening traditions for their inspiration, but they would also look much less modest. Alfred I. du Pont (1864–1935), creator of Nemours, was the eldest son of Eleuthère Irénée and Charlotte Shepherd Henderson from Virginia, both of whom died within a month of each other when the boy was thirteen. Alfred had his first exposure to the French gardening tradition at Eleutherian Mills. Through his many European travels and visits to the great gardens of the continent, he was able to borrow from these garden styles and expand his own vision. Thus Nemours can be seen both as a personal statement of Alfred du Pont as well as an outstanding example of the French gardening tradition as it was passed down through five generations.

In an unpublished research paper, horticulturalist and student of garden history Charles Cresson notes a "striking resemblance" in overall design between Nemours and the Boboli Gardens of the Pitti Palace in Florence, while the colonnades, constructed at Nemours in 1926 as a memorial to Alfred du Pont's grandfather and founder of the family, Pierre Samuel du Pont de Nemours, and his father, Eleuthère Irénée du Pont, are reminiscent of the Gloriette in the Palace of Schonbrunn in Vienna.

But the French influence is paramount. The designs for the tubs of fig trees are those of the great French garden designer of Vaux le Vicomte and Versailles, Andre le Nôtre (1613–1700). In the south garden is the bust of Turgot (1727–1781), minister of finance under Louis XVI. He was a patron of Pierre Samuel's and godfather to his second son, whom he named Eleuthère Irénée in honor of Liberty and Peace. Also in the south garden is the bust of Talleyrand, who had helped Irénée du Pont start his black powder factory.

The three-story, 77-room mansion at Nemours was built between 1909 and 1910 while Alfred du Pont was married to his second wife and cousin, Alicia Bradford (Maddox). The house is in the style of the French chateaux of the period of Louis

Eleutherian Mills, where nature was first subdued with du Pont gardens of practical necessity reflecting European traditions

XVI, the monarch who was beheaded before Pierre Samuel left France with his family in 1799. It has been favorably compared with Le Petit Trianon, considered one of the finest examples of the period. Carrere and Hastings, a New York firm, were the architects, and Smyth and Son, a Wilmington contractor with experience in the Brandywine powder mills, built the mansion to Alfred's exacting specifications. Alicia du Pont's fondness for European styles (she maintained an apartment in Paris) is evident in the fine antiques, rugs, tapestries and portraits that furnish the mansion.

The nine-foot wall surrounding Nemours is a tribute to the craftsmanship of the Brandywine stonemasons, who were forever repairing and constructing the powder mills. It has been said that this wall borrows from French monasteries and medieval walled cities. The cannons near the Love Temple certainly reinforce the notion of fortress rather than garden. They are from the frigate *Constitution* that took part in the War of 1812, which did much to make the Du Pont Company profitable.

On the top of the wall the masons inserted cut glass from thousands of broken bottles brought to the site by the powdermen's children. It has been widely rumored that this wall and these colorful shards symbolize the broken relations between Alfred and other members of the du Pont family. Alfred caused a series of domestic scandals with his various wives and divorces, which shocked his relatives. His cousin Pierre Samuel du Pont, the creator of Longwood, was so disenchanted that he forced Alfred out of any position of power within the company.

Nemours, named for the family home in France, is a celebration of the great French tradition. Longwood, named for the Quaker meetinghouse nearby, which in turn was named for the "Long Woods" that originally forested the area, is a celebration of the American love affair with technology. Both of these houses and gardens were developed over the same period of time by the rival du Pont cousins. With enormous wealth and access to all of the best technology of their time, Alfred and Pierre Samuel du Pont created two strikingly different estates to reflect the personalities of their creators. Pierre S. du Pont (1870–1954) did not build a stately mansion like his cousin Alfred, but chose instead to continue the tradition of modifying an existing house, the Peirce house, to fit his more modest needs. Thus the Peirce-du Pont names are linked to reflect their joint tenure and the decision to embrace an American rather than a European ideal.

George Peirce, an English Quaker from Gloucestershire, arrived in Philadelphia in 1684 and purchased a parcel of 402 acres from William Penn in 1700. In 1703 he gave 200 acres to his oldest daughter Betty, and in 1709 he gave the rest to his son Joshua. Joshua first built a log cabin on the site of the present Peirce house, and in 1730 started construction on the brick house that was eventually to become the Peirce family home.

Nemours can be experienced as a personal statement of Alfred I. du Pont and as an outstanding example of the French gardening tradition

Joshua (1766–1851) and Samuel Peirce (1766–1838), the twin grandsons of Joshua Peirce, started the arboretum to the east of the Peirce-du Pont home in 1798. They created a collector's garden in the tradition of Bartram's Garden, and in time assembled one of this country's finest collections of trees from Europe, Asia and North America.

Samuel Washington Peirce (1814–1880), the bachelor son of Joshua Peirce, inherited the property upon his father's death in 1851 and enriched the plantings with trees and shrubs. He made it more gardenesque with the addition of ornaments that included lifelike iron snakes and frogs. More active involvement in the landscape was encouraged with croquet and boating for his guests. A rustic house and wigwam provided a nostalgic look to an earlier century. Peirce's Park, as it came to be known, was a part of the park movement of the mid-19th century that included Mount Auburn in Boston and Fairmount Park in Philadelphia.

After Samuel Peirce's death in 1880 the property was allowed to decline for about 25 years, changing hands several times. News of a contract to set up a sawmill and log the trees of Peirce's Park was a call to arms for Pierre S. du Pont. The impulse was in the genes, the same impulse that had motivated his great grandfather to wage a campaign to save the Jardins de la République one hundred years before.

When Pierre du Pont purchased Peirce's Park in 1905, he was 35 years old. Four years before, with his cousins Alfred and T. Coleman du Pont, he had rescued the Du Pont Company for about $12 million, although only a couple of thousand dollars actually changed hands. He later applied the same business acumen to rescue this threatened landscape. Pierre du Pont was no newcomer to gardening and had grown up knowing Peirce's Park. Since his mother's death in 1913 he had been looking for a quiet retreat where he could entertain and give full range to his growing appetite for the garden.

Pierre had a fascination with fountains as Alfred had with electricity, and the stunning fountain displays at Longwood are witness to this passion. Conservatories provided the ultimate conquest of space for Pierre, creating environments in which temperature and humidity could be controlled to create tropical paradises in a temperate climate. His interest in these glassed-in gardens can be traced back to his childhood when he first saw the greenhouses constructed by Mathias Baldwin, founder of the Baldwin Locomotive Works, located along Chestnut Street and situated so that passers-by could enjoy the flowers.

In the development of the fountains and conservatories at Longwood, Pierre du Pont drew on the latest technology. As an industrialist, he saw the value of a pilot project and was quick to press what he had learned to full-scale production. He traveled widely, gathering inspiration from around the world, but the style and design of his applications are his own, along with the talented Longwood staff that he assembled.

Although uncompromising in quality and in his attention to detail, Pierre du Pont also had a managerial style that encouraged loyal, long-term associations. He was widely known for his compassion and generosity to his employees, whom he considered to be his "family." Pierre married his first cousin, Alice Belin, late in life and they traveled the world together, fully sharing their love of gardens until Alice died in 1944.

Longwood Gardens was opened to the public in 1946. Pierre du Pont lived on an annuity and leased the gardens back, paying for all of the improvements out of earnings on investment income and capital. The success of his long-range financial planning is amply demonstrated by the years following his death, when the Gardens continued to grow and flourish in accordance with his wishes.

Longwood is such an overpowering experience that one is likely to forget that there is a research and educational side to the operation that have contributed substantially to the garden enterprise of this country. Between 1956 and 1971 thirteen plant-collecting expeditions were sponsored by Longwood Gardens. Hybridization studies on selected groups have also been undertaken as the collections have been curated into one of the largest and finest display gardens in the world. Longwood also offers educational programs, with degrees granted through the University of Delaware.

Winterthur is located within a few miles of the du Pont family seats of Eleutherian Mills, Nemours and Longwood. Its position in the tradition of landscape art, however, is not nearly so close.

Clenny Run, a stream that forms the southern boundary of the garden, immortalizes William Clenny, who acquired the land from William Penn in 1741. Adding to his original holding, Eleuthère Irénée du Pont made a purchase of 169 acres in 1811, part of his farming enterprise that included raising sheep for a developing wool industry on the Brandywine. By 1818 the estate had grown to 450 acres.

In 1834 E. I. du Pont died and in 1837 the property was bought by his son-in-law, James Antoine Bidermann, who in 1816 married Evelina Gabrielle, the second of du Pont's three daughters. Antoine Biderman was the scion of a noted Swiss banking family. His father, Jacques, was a friend of the family founder, Pierre Samuel du Pont, as well as an early investor in the du Pont powder mills. Bidermann had been sent over to check on the Du Pont Company during some rocky times in the early 1800s, and he played an active role in the Du Pont Company from 1815 to 1837, when he retired as president. He then turned his attention to developing the property as a model

Longwood is named for the Long Woods which gave the name to a Quaker Meeting House

farm, and later a pleasure garden. Harking back to his Swiss ancestry, Bidermann chose the name Winterthur from a town located about fifteen miles from Zurich in Switzerland.

In 1867 Henry (the Red) du Pont (1812–1889) purchased the property from James Bidermann, son of Antoine and Evelina. Henry was president of the Du Pont Company from 1850 to 1880 and lived at Eleutherian Mills. He took an active interest in Winterthur, however, primarily by extension of the landholdings, intending the property for his son, Henry Algernon (1838–1926).

Henry Algernon, a graduate of West Point, moved to Winterthur in 1875, a year after his return from his honeymoon in Europe. Although he never served as head of the Du Pont Company, the Colonel, as he was called, was one of its active directors as well as being U.S. Senator from Delaware from 1906 to 1917. He was also a railroad executive and the self-appointed archivist and head of the family in its third generation.

"Kurume" redeemed the blighted land,
An added touch by "Dexter's" hand.
Then "Rock" and "Gable" embellished the hues,
An Azalea Wood to command all views.

Residing on the property, Henry A. du Pont took an active interest in the development of Winterthur. During the period 1885–1925, 900 acres were added to extend farming operations and protect the perimeters from intrusion. His brother-in-law, Theophilus P. Chandler, architect and first dean of the School of Architecture at the University of Pennsylvania, was called upon to assist in the expansion of the manor house. New greenhouses were added, as well as the sunken garden, March Bank and Azalea Woods. Upon his return in 1914 from a trip to Europe with his son, Henry Francis, the Pinetum was planted with encouragement from Charles Sprague Sargent of the Arnold Arboretum.

The Colonel's love of plants was passed along to both his children, Louise Evelina, born in 1877, and Henry Francis, born in 1880. Henry Francis had inherited from his father both his horticultural interests and his talent for strategic and tactical planning, essential qualities for any great garden. He attended the Bussey Institute of Harvard Univesity (class of 1903), where he received formal instruction in horticulture, and he worked closely with his father to develop the gardens of Winterthur. In 1926, upon the death of his father, he inherited the estate which by that time covered an area of 2,400 acres.

Several years after he took over the management of the farm, Henry F. du Pont purchased a foundation herd of Holstein cows from a farmer in Minnesota. His aim was to create a model farm with the Holstein breed as the centerpiece of the operation. He built the finest barns to be found anywhere, launched one of the largest and most successful breeding programs to obtain genetic purity, and retained his own veterinarian on the site. By 1948 the Winterthur herd had won 1,450 advanced registry records in 31 years of consecutive testing.

Henry F. du Pont also brought his considerable collector's instinct to the decorative arts. He rejected the opulence of the Renaissance style in favor of 18th century American antiques and decorative arts, feeling that they had not been given the recognition they deserved. Giving full range to his finely developed eye and sense of strategic planning, he assembled this country's premier collection of American decorative arts and antiques that he installed in rooms rescued from historic homes about to be destroyed.

The relentless pursuit of excellence, the hallmark of the du Ponts in both their business dealings and in their gardens

In 1949 Henry F. du Pont started a catalogue of the collection and hired museum curators to assist in its development, display and interpretation. In 1949 the Winterthur museum opened to the public and in the following year he showed his commitment to education through the establishment of the Winterthur Program in Early American Culture, with degrees granted by the University of Delaware. He died in 1969, having created a garden that offered a lasting legacy for future generations.

We cannot leave Henry F. du Pont without saying something about the professionalism that he brought to his collecting enterprises, not only in the curators of his art and antiques, but also of his gardens. He called himself Winterthur's head gardener, but he was greatly aided in this modest title by Hal Bruce, who came to the gardens in the 1960s and worked with him in his last years. The Winterthur Gardens were opened to the public in 1966 and Hal Bruce's *Winterthur in Bloom*, published in 1968, is one of the outstanding guides to any garden in this country.

The latest offspring in the evolution of du Pont gardens originated with Pamela Cunningham and Lammot du Pont Copeland, who acquired Mount Cuba in 1935. Mount Cuba borrows from earlier traditions and other members of the du Pont family, but here the garden as preserve becomes explicit—a Noah's Ark for the Piedmont flora. Pierre Samuel and Henry Francis du Pont each made contributions to the Copeland estate gardens. Two large yews came as dividends from the topiary garden at Longwood, originally a gift to Pierre from his wife Alice. The atrium at Mount Cuba also bears more than a passing resemblance to the addition of a conservatory at the Peirce House at Longwood. It was Henry F. du Pont, however, who seems to have exerted the greatest influence; in 1952 Lammot du Pont Copeland was elected president of the Winterthur Corporation. He died in 1983.

As an estate garden, Mount Cuba begins as many such gardens, first as foundation plantings of trees and shrubs to frame the manor house, then enhanced by terraces and garden rooms. Pamela Copeland's interest in gardening can be traced back to her childhood in Litchfield, Connecticut, with her botanist mother. She also absorbed the lessons that were given by other du Ponts and the landscape architects who were commissioned to work at Mount Cuba, including Marian Coffin (1876–1957), whose ideas she followed in planting sweeps of a single species to create a dramatic effect. Here is a garden that has progressed from the marigolds that the owner first planted as a newlywed to the golden alexanders (*Zizia aurea*) that grow widely through the Piedmont region. Mount Cuba represents the most recent stage of metamorphosis of the du Pont gardens from amenity horticulture to the preservation of a flora.

The du Pont family became successful because of a combination of factors— imaginative leadership, luck, a mixture of black powder and the timing and frequency of wars in the 19th century. But consistent with the physiocratic ideals of true wealth being vested in land, a significant portion of the du Pont wealth was spent in agricultural pursuits. As the successes of the Du Pont Company were compounded, the du Pont gardens became one of the primary means of exhibiting wealth, and a strong current of *noblesse oblige* that coursed through the family resulted in these great estates opening to the public. What sets the du Pont gardens apart is their consistent high quality and monumental scale. These gardens of practicality, pleasure and preserve represent some of our greatest aspirations about the human condition and our place in nature.

News of a contract to set up a sawmill and log the trees of Peirce's Park was a call to arms for Pierre S. du Pont

Eleutherian Mills was sited in the naturally wooded landscape of the Brandywine River

Hagley Museum and Library

. . . Being without a garden was the greatest deprivation; and it is the first thing that occupied my time.

Letter from E. I. DU PONT in 1803

Mill race at Hagley

THE HAGLEY MUSEUM AND LIBRARY is located in the picturesque Brandywine River Valley. Situated in the naturally wooded, riparian landscape, the area was first settled by the Lenni Lenape Indians, and later by the Swedes, Dutch and British before the Americans finally won their independence. The 230-acre Eleutherian and Hagley Mills site is the cradle of the great du Pont public gardens: Alfred I. du Pont's Nemours, Pierre S. du Pont's Longwood and Henry Francis du Pont's Winterthur.

Eleuthère Irénée du Pont had received his formal introduction to the botanical sciences at the Jardin des Plantes in Paris before coming to this country in 1800. As founder of the Du Pont Company, he arranged for others in his employ to collect seeds and exchange plants. His garden at Eleutherian Mills, less than two acres in size, could be considered one of the early collector's gardens.

Unlike the collector's gardens of Bartram or the Painter brothers (who planted the Tyler Arboretum), however, Irénée du Pont's garden was planted in the French style, with parterres and espaliered trees. Designed to please the palate as well as the eye, it had vegetables and fruits mixed with herbs, shrubs and many kinds of flowers, especially roses. Architectural features were added—a pump in 1811, a latticework summerhouse in 1817, a greenhouse in 1822. After Irénée's death in 1834, his daughter Victorine continued to refine the garden until 1890, when an explosion struck the Eleutherian Powder Mills and the du Ponts vacated the house.

The manufacture of gunpowder stopped at Eleutherian Mills in the 1920s and the prop-

Narrow gauge rail tracks at Hagley

erty was purchased from the Du Pont Company in 1923 by Henry Algernon du Pont, grandson of the founder, for his daughter Louise Evelina (1877–1958), wife of Francis B. Crowninshield, yachtsman and one of Theodore Roosevelt's Rough Riders. Louise and Francis Crowninshield transformed the powder mill into a romantic ruin garden.

In what must be the least likely of sites, a black powder mill, a place we are more likely to associate with war and destruction, a garden rises, Phoenix-like, out of the ashes. Mythic heroes of Aphrodite, Pan, Mercury, Jason and Minerva accent the Italianate architec-

ture of the Crowninshield garden. Tunnels originally used to transfer powder have been converted into grottoes.

One of the original members of the National Trust for Historic Preservation, and an active garden club member, Louise du Pont Crowninshield deeded the property in 1952 to establish the Eleutherian Mills-Hagley Foundation. The main garden has been restored to the period of 1803–1834 by William H. Frederick, a well-known landscape architect and garden writer of the region. The Crowninshield garden has been closed since 1960, but plans have been made to restore it. Based on re-

For E. I. du Pont, as for Thomas Jefferson, trees represented "an indestructible source of wealth"

search by one of the Longwood Fellows, a 19th century workman's garden is also being developed on this site.

The Hagley Museum and Library, an independent, non-profit corporation, was founded in 1952 on the 150th anniversary of the Du Pont Company as a testimonial to the belief that "there is no privilege that is not inseparably bound to duty." This inscription appears on a monument placed on the Brandywine during the 150th anniversary celebrations.

The mansion and gardens are a legacy of the great French architectural and gardening traditions

Nemours

If I could do what I wanted I'd build a house

under those trees and sit down and read books

and eat ice cream the rest of my life.

E. I. DU PONT to his son Alfred

A RECREATION of French chateau country is located north of Wilmington off Rockland Road. This 300-acre estate was the residence of Alfred I. du Pont (1864–1935), musician and mechanical wizard, powderman and inventor, political and social engineer, financier and humanitarian.

The mansion and gardens are a legacy of the great French architectural and gardening traditions which were part of Alfred I. du Pont's heritage and a part of his experience in having grown up on the Brandywine River around Eleutherian Mills. With its powerful geometry, celebrating control over nature, the French gardening style was perfectly suited to Alfred's analytical way of thinking and his own substantial mechanical gifts.

A visit to the garden should begin at the mansion, preferably on the second or third floors looking down at the garden; French gardens were designed for a heavenly perspective. To the west, the grand design is laid out like the axle of some giant machine, one third of a mile long. It is anchored on the east by the mansion and on the west by the Love Temple, with its statue of Diana, Goddess of the Hunt, by Jean Antoine Houdon (1741–1828). The reflecting pool with its fountains, colonnades and sunken gardens interrupts the axle with geometric precision. The maze garden is slightly tilted, a device employed to correct for optical distortion.

The English gates were constructed in 1488 for Wimbledon Manor, a house given by Henry VIII to his sixth wife, Catherine Parr, in 1543. The Russian gates were made for Catherine the Great's palace outside St. Petersburg. The dates on the gate (1729–1796) are those of Catherine II, Empress of Russia.

The reflecting pool with its fountain, colonnades and sunken gardens interrupts the axis with geometric precision

The colonnade has been compared with the Glorietta in the Palace of Schonbrun in Vienna

The two marble sphinxes on the front terrace of the house were presented by Louis XIV (1638–1715) to Colbert (1619–1683). They bear the face of Louise de la Valliere, one of Louis XIV's mistresses. They originally stood in the gardens of Sceaux, Colbert's chateau, destroyed during the French Revolution. It was Louis XVI who granted Pierre Samuel du Pont de Nemours a title for his contributions to the peace treaty of 1783. The family crest with the lion of France on the left and the eagle on the right are bracketed by the motto *Rectitudine Sto* (By Uprightness I stand).

Alfred du Pont grew up in the Brandywine powder yards and played with powdermen's children. He had three children by his first wife, Bessie Gardner, and one of the great tragedies of his life was the estrangement that he suffered from his children after his divorce in 1906. After he married his third wife, Jessie D. Ball, in 1921, however, he became reconciled to his own children and to a number of du Pont cousins as well. The vestiges of this interest in children and animals can still be found throughout the gardens. The Wren's Nest southwest of the colonnades was used as a schoolhouse and playhouse by the estate children. The early 20th century figurines that appear in the rock garden to the west of the colonnades and about halfway down to the Love Temple are from Czechoslovakia and portray a whimsical nature that pleases both children and adults.

Alfred's particular fondness for animals

In the charging streams, waterwheels, mirrored pools, canals and cooling fountains, Alfred I. du Pont's particular brand of genius for mechanics is clearly shown

finds expression in several of the garden sculptures. The two elk at the top of the vista are the work of Prosper Lecourtier (1855–1924), who specialized in animal sculpture. Dogs were Alfred's particular favorites, however. The bloodhounds by Jean de Sommevoire and *Naturae Primus Impetus* (First Instinct of Nature), by A. Durene, of a bull mastiff protecting her pups, are objects that a true dog lover would collect and place in the garden.

Growing up on the Brandywine and spending 18 years in the powder yard, Alfred worked to perfect the ways water moves wheels, belts and rollers to make black powder. It was natural then that water would occupy a central place in his garden. In the charging streams, waterwheels, mirrored pools, canals and cooling fountains, Alfred du Pont's particular brand of genius for mechanics is clearly shown. The "Four Seasons" around the Reflecting Pool are by Henri Crenier (1873–1948).

In the French gardening tradition, we think of water under control, conformed to the absolute will of the designer. That is clearly the overall impression that one gains from a look down the main axis of Nemours. Near the end of that axis, however, between the colonnades and the Love Temple, is a chain of ponds that take a naturalistic form. The requirement for absolute control is eased to allow the natural grace of water to be expressed, recalling the English school of landscape gardening of William Kent, Capability Brown and Humphry Repton. It is at this chain of pools, constantly under refinement during Alfred's lifetime, where the French and English gardening traditions intersect, vividly expressing the conjunction of Alfred's American and French ancestry in this cross-cultural garden.

The sunken gardens were designed by Alfred Victor du Pont and Gabriel Messena. Victor, Alfred's son by his first wife, left the du Pont firm, with his father's blessing, to study architecture in Europe; their correspondence contains abundant references to his design for the gardens. The walls and steps are travertine marble from Rome. Charles Sarrabezolles (born 1888) sculpted the main statuary at the top and the side statues in the fountains. Claude Grange (1890–1971) did the marble statues at the top of the steps and the bronzes in the pools.

Nemours was opened to the public in 1977 and is managed and directed by the Nemours Foundation. The A. I. du Pont Institute is the joint project of Alfred and his wife, Jessie. Together they planned the Nemours Foundation and hospital as instruments to carry out their humanitarian desires and belief that wealth should be applied in the service of mankind.

OPPOSITE: *Anchoring the west end of the axis, The Temple of Love*

Conservatories provided the ultimate conquest of space for Pierre S. du Pont

Longwood Gardens

... Captivating beyond description with jets of all kinds spurting like mad and without cease. I could have remained all day beside this pool in Machinery Hall.

PIERRE S. DU PONT
at the Centennial Exposition, 1876

LONGWOOD GARDENS is located in the rolling hills of the Brandywine Valley, thirty miles west of Philadelphia in Kennett Square, Pennsylvania. Nowhere can the transformation of nature into the art of the garden be experienced so comprehensively and so grandly as at Longwood Gardens, the extraordinary creation of Pierre Samuel du Pont (1870–1954).

Five generations of Peirces, a Quaker farming family, first began to bend nature to their will on these premises and later embellish it to create one of the early pleasure gardens of this country. It was a self-confessed "non-working Episcopalian," however, acting president of Du Pont in 1907 and later Chairman of General Motors, Pierre Samuel du Pont, who transformed the Peirce garden into a horticultural masterpiece on a royal scale. Unlike the playgrounds designed for the aristocracy, however, this captain of industry in a democratic society had in mind a garden "for the sole use of the public for purposes of exhibition, instruction, education and enjoyment."

The name, Longwood, is taken from the Quaker meetinghouse built in 1859 located a few miles to the south of the Gardens. That name originates from the earlier "Long Woods," the deciduous hardwood forests that greeted William Penn and the Colonial settlers, remnants of which can still be found to the north of the conservatories and along the western side of the gardens. The American chestnut is gone but mighty specimens of tulip poplar, oak and hickory still invest these woods. The meadows and fields were carved from these forests for crops and pasturage in colonial days; today they are managed for their displays of wildflowers.

A place where nature could be manipulated to intensify the enjoyment one could take in the landscape

Always to Pierre S. du Pont's exacting standard to do each garden project in a "first-class way"

Angel's Trumpet, Datura versicolor

The Peirce place was a frequently visited arboretum in the second half of the 19th century. Vestiges of the original formal allees can still be seen in the 200-year-old ginkgo (*Ginkgo biloba*), cucumber tree (*Magnolia acuminata*) and Kentucky coffee tree (*Gymnocladus dioica*). The Peirce-du Pont house is open to visitors and a must for those wishing to find the historical roots of this garden.

In 1905 the property was purchased by Pierre du Pont to save the Peirces' trees. A sawmill was being set up to scavenge the arboretum and on hearing of this, Pierre du Pont nobly stepped in to save it from this terrible fate. The year following his purchase, he started his own sculpting of the site. He designed a flower garden walk below the Peirce-du Pont house that was terminated with a 20-foot circular fountain.

Pierre du Pont's interest in fountains began when he was taken as a child of six to the Centennial in 1876 and saw "jets of all kinds spurting like mad and without cease." This fascination grew with his trips to Paris in 1889 when he first saw Versailles, and the 1893 World's Columbian Exposition in Chicago where, in the Court of Honor, he first witnessed illuminated fountains. A visit to Villa Gamberaia in 1925 inspired the Italian Water Fountain that was completed in 1927. The success of this fountain and the installation of others in the open-air theater that had been started in 1912 encouraged Pierre to undertake even more monumental projects. The main fountains in front of the conservatory were started in 1928 and completed in 1931. The illuminated hydraulic technology is controlled by electronic systems to create one of the most magnificent

Cockscomb, Celosia "Fordhook"

Weeping Willow, Salix babylonica

fountain displays to be found anywhere in the world. Computerized controls were added in 1984.

In 1914 the first greenhouses at Longwood Gardens were constructed by connecting two wings of the Peirce-du Pont house, thus forming a conservatory. The success of this first venture led to the planning from 1916 to 1917 of greatly expanded conservatories. After World War I, President Woodrow Wilson added a patriotic motive, if one was needed, by encouraging major public works projects to re-tool American industry and employ the labor force in peaceful pursuits. Pierre happily obliged and the main conservatories were completed in 1921.

The technology for these conservatories was state-of-the-art. A series of gigantic boilers, designed with back-up systems, provide the heat, all artfully concealed so as not to intrude upon the exhibition of the plants. Today more than 4,500 kinds of plants are grown in twenty indoor gardens, offering one of the best introductions to the variety of plants to be seen anywhere.

In the tradition of his French heritage, Pierre created one of the most spectacular open-air theaters of this country. He started his annual June parties in 1909, and the addition of fountains and lights and a water curtain all added to the delight of his guests and the general public. No garden which represents itself as living theater, however, would be without music. Pierre's interest in music can be traced to his mother, who played the organ and piano. Pierre was at one time even a member of his cousin Alfred's band. The music room off the main conservatory was de-

In the topiary elephant a bit of whimsy to delight children of all ages

signed by J. Walter Cope and built in 1923. Pierre du Pont purchased an Aeolian organ and subsequently enlarged it, but it did not prove up to his high standards. In 1929 he contracted with Aeolian to construct what may well be the world's largest residential organ. It was designed by Firmin Swinnen, a widely-acclaimed Belgian organist, who served as organist in residence at Longwood from 1923 until 1956. Today, there are about 150 organ and choral concerts during December, and guest artists come from all over the world to play this magnificent instrument.

But in the more modest sundial, located in the topiary garden, this industrial genius showed the range of his interests. The sundial project started, as did many of Pierre du Pont's projects, as a challenge to press technology to its limits. Sundials that could be ordered off the shelf were simply not accurate enough. In the end the staff took sightings of the sun at noon each day to work out the precise equations for the analemma, the figure-eight scale on which the shadow is cast by the gnomon and from which the time is taken. This rather modest-looking, ancient instrument took six to eight years to produce, longer than the main conservatory!

How fitting that the final project during Pierre du Pont's lifetime should be to undertake the challenge of bending the rays of the sun to his own rigorous demands for accuracy. The drive for perfection continues. In recent years, the equations of the analemma were recalculated to produce an instrument that would give accuracy to two minutes.

Garden features added since Pierre's death include the Lily Display Garden (1957), New Entrance (1964), Palm House (1966), Eye of Water (1968), East Conservatory (1973) and a Terrace Garden Restaurant (1983). The services of distinguished landscape gardener and University of Pennsylvania professor Sir Peter Shepheard have been retained as a designer and consultant on several of these projects. Major collections of orchids, insectivorous

Sacred Lotus, Nelumbo nucifera

The lily display garden was added in 1957

plants, palms, water lilies and heaths have also been added to the gardens. Special display gardens designed for their instructional purposes have also been added.

Longwood Gardens is a private, non-profit corporation, with 180 full-time employees including 70 gardeners, and 80 part-time employees to maintain the 1,000-acre tract of land, 350 acres of which are open to the public.

"I want a thing going, have it established, and see it going. Then I'll know that what I want is to be done."

HENRY F. DU PONT

Winterthur Museum, Garden, Library

My work is in the garden.

HENRY FRANCIS DU PONT

A. P. Saunders brought together at Winterthur peonies from Eastern Europe, the Himalayas and the Caucasus

SIX MILES northwest of Wilmington, Delaware, the entrance drive brings visitors through the rolling farmland and woods of the Brandywine Valley across Clenny Run to Winterthur. This 60-acre garden on the 1,000-acre estate has been in du Pont ownership since 1811, and reflects Henry Francis du Pont's (1880–1969) preference for the informal style of gardening.

Unlike Longwood or Nemours, Winterthur draws its inspiration directly from nature. The gardens tell a story of how the forests of the Brandywine first were sculpted into productive farmland, the farmland metamorphosed into pleasure garden, and in time, the entire landscape conserved as a work of landscape art. And while Henry Francis du Pont gained a wide reputation as a breeder of Holstein cattle and collector of American antiques, one experiences him most as an artist in the garden.

Upon arriving at the parking lot, instead of heading directly for the visitors' pavilion, step back in time into Chandler's Woods, located across the lot from the entrance to the main gardens. Listen to the distant echo of woods that once greeted William Penn. Some of the trees in this woodland are more than 300 years old. Hillsides have been planted with native mountain laurel (*Kalmia latifolia*), the generic name commemorating the Swedish botanist, Peter Kalm, who was sent to this country by fellow-botanist and countryman, Linnaeus. Paths were cut through these woods in 1963 and the area opened to the public almost ten years after Henry du Pont's death.

The Azalea Woods, located in the main part of the garden, were created from the

The gardens tell a story of how the forests of the Brandywine were sculpted into productive farmland

gaping holes left in the canopies after the Chestnut blight struck the area in 1911. Kurume azaleas, first introduced at the San Francisco World's Fair in 1915, were planted in the 1920s when the work on the Azalea Woods was under way. The Dexter and Gable hybrids were added in the 1930s, and most of what is seen today laid out in the mid-1940s. Henry du Pont had a lifelong love affair with azaleas; it is the most widely-used plant at Winterthur. The season begins with the flowering of the *Rhododendron micronulatum* and ends with the *Rhododendron discolor*.

In 1927 the *Corylopsis/Chaemomeles* Walks were planted. There are 67 species of Oak in America. In the 1950s plantings went out on Oak Hill to feature the many contributions of this group to the landscape. A noted hybridizer of peonies, Professor A. P. Saunders

of Clinton, New York, brought together the germplasm of the peonies from Eastern Europe, the Himalayas and the Caucasus to create an outstanding collection of new forms that were incorporated into Henry du Pont's Peony Garden in the early 1940s.

In the late 1920s the reflecting pools and terrace gardens, designed by landscape architect Marian Coffin, were installed east of the house. As family interests changed, the tennis and croquet courts were converted by Marian Coffin into the sundial garden. This area is about as close as Winterthur comes to a formal garden.

The abandoned quarry was converted into a garden room in the 1960s and in May and June features an outstanding grouping of primroses. A galaxy of flowering shrubs in-

The azalea woods, located in the main part of the garden, were created from the gaping holes left in the canopies after the chestnut blight struck the area in 1911

One experiences Henry F. du Pont most as an artist in his garden at Winterthur

cluding *Stewartia*, *Styrax*, lilacs and *Deutzia*, were selected for summer interest and planted in the area of the sycamores at the eastern extremity of the garden. Collections of *Lilium*, ferns, *Clematis*, *Primula*, *Chionanthus*, *Kalmia*, *Liriope* and *Hamamelis* form ensembles to extend seasonal interest.

Henry du Pont assembled his American decorative arts and garden collections as part of an integrated composition—something to be lived in. He saw the garden as a series of rooms to be furnished and decorated like the rooms in his Museum. Corridors were not to be barren hallways but rather embellished with colors and textures as they were in his

house. He wanted to preserve "windows" in his garden rooms to provide vistas, and signs in the garden read "This view should forever be preserved." (Part of that view would originally have been the pedigree herds of black and white Holstein cattle that Henry du Pont collected along with his furniture and plants.)

As testimony to the farsightedness of Henry du Pont, in 1930 Winterthur was chartered as a non-profit charitable and educational foundation in the state of Delaware. In 1951 Henry du Pont conveyed to the Winterthur Corporation his ancestral home and the surrounding property, which were opened to the public in 1966.

Mount Cuba's landscape began as foundation plantings around the manor house and then reached out to the woodlands and fields beyond

Mount Cuba

Open space will be just as valuable as
looking at antiques in fifty years.

MRS. LAMMOT DU PONT COPELAND

OFF BARLEY MILL ROAD, along Red
Clay Creek northwest of Wilmington,
Delaware, is the 230-acre estate of Pamela
Cunningham and Lammot du Pont Copeland.
Mount Cuba was acquired in the mid-1930s
when the Copelands moved from Connecticut
to Delaware, where Lammot would begin his
climb up the du Pont corporate ladder, eventually to become president in 1962.

Mount Cuba was named for the village of
Mount Cuba, which was originally called
"Cuba Rock" by an Irish settler in 1730. As a
relatively recent addition to the du Pont gardens, Mount Cuba has connected with the
conservation movement and is being developed as a refuge and research center for the
Piedmont flora. The Piedmont is that hilly upland region of the Eastern United States, between the Atlantic coastal plain and the Appalachian mountains. More than 3,000 species
of plants have been identified in this region,
and many have been placed on the threatened
or endangered list.

The hilly countryside of the Brandywine
unfolds as the road climbs Mount Cuba, a
high point botanically, horticulturally and
topographically in Delaware. That this is a
plant person's garden is evident from the extensive terraced rock garden cut into the bank
to the left of the road. It is an outstanding
demonstration of what can be done to convert
a raw roadside into a floral delight. The first
plans for this garden were developed by Upper Bank Nurseries a year after the Copelands
moved into their new home.

The manor house commanding the hill is
Virginia Georgian in its architectural style. It

Showing progress in gardening from the marigolds first planted as newlyweds to the Golden Alexanders (Zizia aurea) that grow widely through the Piedmont region

was designed by Samuel and Victorine Homsey (Victorine was a cousin of Lammot Copeland), and built between 1936 and 1937. The Homseys were engaged on several du Pont garden projects: the Palm House, Cactus House, the restaurant at Longwood, and the Pavilion at Winterthur. Henry F. du Pont encouraged the Copelands in the purchase of antiques and paneled rooms from southern mansions in which to house them. He gave them the lead cistern in the garden, and in the woodland gardens there is a shared interest in native plants and the informal garden style.

Mount Cuba, however, is more than just an echo of Winterthur located about two miles to the east. Several prominent Philadelphia landscape architects have plied their trade here. Thomas W. Sears, a product of Harvard and member of the Olmsted Brothers firm in Brookline, Massachusetts, worked at Mount Cuba from 1936 to 1938. The mature trees surrounding the house, ginkgo, umbrella pine, Chinese toon and Katsura (*Cercidiphyllum japonicum*) are all testimony to his commitment to bring variety into his landscapes. The forecourt, south terrace, lilac path, gum trees and cutting garden also date to the Sears era and make up the foundation for the formal garden.

Upon the recommendation of Henry du Pont, Marian Coffin began working at Mount Cuba in the late 1940s. The winter hazels (*Corylopsis*) and Korean rhododendrons as underplantings are reminiscent of Winterthur. The South Terrace borders of Ghent and Mollis azaleas were designed by this respected landscape architect. At the same time, she relocated one half of the sweet gums (*Liquidambar*) planted by Thomas Sears to create an allee along the Terrace. She designed the round garden with bordering beds that change with the seasons, and swimming pool in the shape of a Maltese Cross.

The purchase of 20.5 acres bordering the estate in the 1950s made it possible to start what was first referred to as Mount Cuba Botanical Park. Another Harvard-trained landscape architect and classmate of Lammot Copeland, Seth Kelsey, assisted with the development of this part of the estate from 1965 to 1971. After the land had been cleared and paths cut through the woods, in 1966 construction of the four ponds was started. The high canopy of Tulip trees gives majesty to the woods filled with such delights as Dutchman's breeches (*Dicentra cucullaria*), Bloodroot (*Sanguinaria canadensis*) and rue-anemone (*Anemonella thalictroides*). The trails have been planted with over one hundred species of the Piedmont flora, all carefully labeled.

In the 1970s the formal gardens were embellished through the work of another prominent Delaware landscape architect, William H. Frederick. Frederick was president of the board of Longwood Gardens, Inc., from 1970 to 1980, and author of restoration plans for the garden of Eleuthère Irénée du Pont at Hagley Mills. In the early 1980s Frederick contributed the design of the East Terrace with its crimson barberry.

Mount Cuba is a private estate open by appointment only for horticultural groups, but plans are afoot to open it more frequently. In 1983 Dr. Richard Lighty, a well-known local horticulturalist and one-time director of the Longwood Program, was appointed director of the renamed Mount Cuba Center. The plan here is to protect the site and carry out the garden's mission—the appreciation and conservation of the Piedmont flora. To this end, the Center is propagating cultivars of horticultural interest and releasing them to the nursery trade. This has resulted in such gems as *Heuchera* "Palace Purple," whose wine red leaves make such a lovely addition to modern gardens public and private.

The most recent stage in the evolution of du Pont gardens—from amenity horticulture to the preservation of the Piedmont flora

Chapter 6

From Private Gardens
to Public Parks

Logan Square

OVERLEAF: *Logan Square*

*T*HE "GREENE COUNTRY TOWNE" proved to be one of William Penn's most important and enduring ideas. It was an idea first stamped upon the land according to the mandates Penn had given his Surveyor, Captain Thomas Holmes. In 1683 Holmes drew the grid for the city of Philadelphia that guided future development along North/South (Broad Street) and East/West (Market Street) axes. "The streets were laid off by marking their course through the primitive forest by blazing the trees," according to the chronicler of the Centennial Exhibition, James McCabe. A ten-acre Center Square, where City Hall now stands, was placed at the intersection of this axis, approximately equidistant from the Delaware and Schuylkill Rivers. Wooded squares of about seven acres anchored each of the quadrants. William Penn's idea of a city drew its essential character from a God-centered Nature. The embodiment of that idea was in time to become Philadelphia's greatest treasure—Fairmount Park.

The idea of breaking out of the constraints of the original grid design and connecting the heart of the city (Penn's Square) with the park beyond surfaced shortly after the Civil War. The idea gained momentum toward the end of the 19th century and eventually led to the Benjamin Franklin Parkway, the gateway to Fairmount Park that has been described by art historian David Brownlee as "America's first important contribution to urban design."

Washington, Franklin, Rittenhouse and Logan Squares in Thomas Holmes's original plan have each evolved a character of their own as they accommodated to the changing needs of bartering spaces, burying places, hunting grounds and gallows. Bearing the names of the nation's and city's founding fathers, they link other places and times to tell the story of Philadelphia's gardening tradition. They were added to Fairmount Park in 1915.

But the central theme of the story of Fairmount Park is water. In 1801, on the site where City Hall now stands, was a small neoclassical building designed by Benjamin Henry Latrobe (1764–1820) that housed a steam engine to pump water into a small reservoir for redistribution through a system of wooden pipes. Twenty years later, a student of Latrobe's, Frederick Graff (1774–1847), was hired to find a better solution. By the last decade of the 18th century, recurrent epidemics of yellow fever had implicated the water supply and convinced the city fathers that a larger and safer supply was needed if the city was to grow and prosper. Graff looked to the high ground, William Penn's Faire Mount, and built there in 1812 an elevated reservoir amidst five landscaped acres to provide Philadelphia with water.

After the city was founded the residents quickly found ways to break the gridlock and explore the surrounding countryside. As wealth from trade and the beginnings of manufacture increased, stately homes sprouted on the ridge overlooking the Schuylkill River in the section of the Park that is East River (Kelly) Drive. Some of these estates, Laurel Hill, Woodford, Mt. Pleasant, Strawberry Mansion and Lemon Hill, date to the mid and late 18th century and were the summer homes of some of the most powerful and influential families of this country. Sadly, little remains of their splendid gardens.

In the West Park section of Fairmount we can best trace the transformation of the garden enterprise from farmstead and stately home with pleasure garden to public park. Here we see the assertion of Philadelphia as the preeminent horticultural center of this nation and a people becoming increasingly sensitive to the value of wilderness. America's first zoological garden was founded in West Park in 1874. And here a young nation flexed its muscles to stage a great international exhibition in celebration of its first hundred years.

The mid-19th century saw great technological advancement resulting in the accumulation of enormous wealth. But that industrial progress had substantial social costs attached: a growing disparity between the classes with widespread poverty and misery. The tale of Philadelphia had become one of the old town, constricted by the original grid, metamorphosing into an industrial city, in order to keep from being swallowed up by a burgeoning suburb that was running out of control.

The ideals of the "greene Country Towne" were to be woven into the warp and woof of the new industrial city. On September 15, 1855, an ordinance was passed establishing Fairmount Park. The estate of Lemon Hill, already purchased by the city in 1844 to protect the water supply and later run as a beer garden along with the gardens around the waterworks, was adopted as Fairmount's first official public land. Sections of West Park were added in 1866.

Philadelphia Zoo

An Act of the General Assembly passed on March 26, 1867, authorized the city to purchase land "to be laid out and maintained forever as an open public place and park, for the health and enjoyment of the people of the said City, and the preservation of the water supply." To implement this Act the Fairmount Park Commission was organized on June 3, 1867, and the Fairmount Park Art Association was founded five years later. These two groups were charged with organizing the Centennial celebrations, an event that established the spirit of 1876 as part of the Victorian spirit of optimism, pride in the present and hope for the future.

After the 1867 Act was passed, the acquisition of land for the direct benefit of the public became a prime objective. On April 14, 1868, a supplementary bill was passed that provided funds to purchase land for public use. With these legal tools in hand the city had the means needed both to rake in the land and dig into the pockets of the citizenry. The seeds of Philadelphia's urban park were ready to be broadcast into the suburbs.

Franklin Square

The urban park movement, promoted by Andrew Jackson Downing towards the end of the first half of the 19th century and taken up by Frederick Law Olmsted in the second half, would make a new and explicit statement about parks as instruments of achieving social order. Laurel Hill Cemetery and Peirce's Park near Kennett Square foreshadowed this movement, which eventually led to the creation of Central Park in New York, Lincoln Park in Chicago, Golden Gate Park in San Francisco and Brooklyn's Prospect Park. The newly-formed Fairmount Park Commission consulted Olmsted about their park's development, and its basic design is commonly credited to him. But it was Hermann Joseph Schwartzman (1843–1891), an ex-officer in the Royal Bavarian Army who had immigrated to America in 1868, who actually guided the planning of the park.

The several major themes that defined Fairmount Park were all established by the end of the 19th century: the protection of stream corridors, the creation of parks for recreational purposes and the preservation of historic sites. Philadelphia led the way in the creation of the largest park within a city limit in America. (It was three times as large as Central Park.) With the acquisition of acreage along the Schuylkill River to prevent pollution and drainage problems, and with the East and West Parks in hand, the Commission was ready to spawn new parks upstream. The desire to extend the protection of the water supply, the health-giving qualities of the park and the practical consideration of developing a closer link with the successful Germantown and Chestnut Hill suburbs were all lures to bring the Commission north and westward to create one of the most remarkable sections of the park.

By the end of the first decade of the 20th century, Fairmount Park had grown to 75 percent of its present size and four of the six major stream corridors that either bounded or traversed the city were wrapped in the protective custody of the Fairmount Park Commission. The Commission was ready to enlarge the possibilities by adding historic sites, expanding recreational facilities and eventually taking custody of all the city's street trees.

The East and West Park areas with their priceless assortment of colonial houses were brought under Park management shortly after Fairmount Park was established in 1867. The historic Rittenhouse Mills were acquired in the 1870s and are being restored as a mill community. Bartram's Garden along the Schuylkill was acquired in

1891 and Penn Treaty Park along the Delaware in 1894. The acquisition of historic properties continued through much of the early 20th century through the appropriation of the four original squares in 1915, and Christ Church, 1928. The towpath trailing along 120 acres of Manayunk Canal that carried raw materials used in manufacturing and contributed to the pollution that stimulated the Park's early development, was acquired in 1979.

Increasingly the Park has seen its mission expanded into one or more active community involvements and into education. The Andorra and Pennypack Nature Centers are signs of increasing environmental concern. The acquisition of the 88-acre Fox Chase Farm in 1975 and the 76-acre Manatawna Farm in 1983 are an attempt to preserve lifestyles that have disappeared from urban areas.

Fairmount Park has been shaped by the transformation of a city from country town to industrial city. Its land area has been shaped by design and luck, some good, some bad—astute dealing, high hopes and low political ambition. The several themes that launched the park are still being played out today: stream protection, cultural amenity, repository for the city's cultural history, purveyor of recreational experience and educational facilities.

The Philadelphia Zoological Society was founded in 1859 and the Zoological Garden opened its gates in the West Park section of Fairmount in 1874. With the threats of loss of diversity and increasing difficulties in importing animals, the Philadelphia Zoo, like all zoos and aquaria, has placed an increasing emphasis on breeding studies of rare and endangered animals. Experiential learning is provided in the Children's Petting Zoo, and also in the "Tree House," originally designed by Philadelphia architects Frank Furness and George Hewitt as an exhibit for hoofed animals. Within this richly-ornamented Victorian building, restored and readapted in 1985 by the distinguished Philadelphia firm of Venturi Rauch and Scott Brown, is a four-story, fiberglass replica of a fig tree, with other fantastic exhibits that please both children and adults.

The idea that college campuses should also be regarded as public parks was first expressed by Martha Carey Thomas, dean from 1885 to 1895 and president from 1895 to 1922 of Bryn Mawr College. Walter Cope and John Stewardson were responsible for the Tudor Gothic style of architecture on the campus, and two of this country's

Woodland Cemetery

most noted landscape architects, Calvert Vaux and Frederick Law Olmsted, had a hand in planning the gardens, which offer an education in horticulture, as well as the art of landscaping, to the students of the college.

The idea of college campus as public park was taken up by several other colleges in the area. The Olmstedian park design drawn up for Bryn Mawr by Vaux and Company in 1884, with curving roads and buildings arranged in a quadrangle, resembles that which we find on the Haverford College campus.

The development of the American College campus also followed the Bryn Mawr concept. Largely designed by Harry Wood, the campus features many fine specimen trees and shrubs. These landscapes were formed not only as an integrated work of art and a research tool for an educational institution, but they serve as a model of the institution's gift to the community—the college campus as community park.

Awbury Arboretum is home to five generations of Copes, a prominent Quaker mercantile family. Fifteen houses of architectural merit are scattered over the grounds, thanks to Walter Cope, in partnership with John Stewardson, whose work can be seen not only at Bryn Mawr, but on university campuses around the country—Princeton, the University of Pennsylvania and Washington University in St. Louis.

William Draper Lewis, Dean of Penn's Law School and a Cope in-law, set up the legal mechanisms to transfer this privately-held Quaker space to public open space, stressing its purpose as an educational park and arboretum "in connection with the study of landscape gardening, trees, shrubs, flowers and birds." Like few other places, the Awbury Arboretum reflects the profound changes which have taken place in the landscape over the past 150 years. It is a test case of how private, even cloistered existence can survive the spread of urbanization and attendant blight. Today a part of the grounds are given over to a thriving community garden, sponsored by Temple University's urban garden program.

Woven through the tapestry of gardens, canopied plazas and varied landscape plantings that make up Independence National Historical Park are several messages. The thread of garden history can be traced here as nowhere else in the country: parterred colonial gardens, expansive mall and symbolic garden of Franklin Court bracketed by two of Penn's original squares. These varied open spaces are symbolic of the various views of the past and present that must be reconciled in an urban context.

Independence Park reflects the problems connected with great growth and change as our attitudes towards the environment become more sensitive. Philadelphia had grown up around a scattering of buildings of national historic significance. The challenge was how to enshrine them. Countless battle plans for preservation were drawn up through the 1950s and 1960s, alliances forged and compromises negotiated. In the end it was to be a mixed strategy, one that would give rise to a totally new conception for an urban park. It is a long way from Penn's original vision of a "greene Country Towne," but it attempts to combine the needs of the people with the need to achieve a lasting balance with nature.

OPPOSITE: *Fairmount Park*

The Franklin Institute, Academy of Natural Science and Free Library rim Logan Square to make this one of the country's major hubs of history and education

Fairmount Park

Somewhere in its 8,700 acres is an example of practically every important idea about parks, recreation, and landscape gardening formulated in the past 300 years.

FAIRMOUNT PARK MASTERPLAN,
December 14, 1983

WASHINGTON SQUARE

Washington Square, located in the southeast quadrant between 6th and 7th and Walnut and Locust Streets, began as a pasture and grew into a canopied space with large sycamore, oak, catalpa and basswood. It was a cemetery for Revolutionary War soldiers and some who died of yellow fever in 1793. Now presided over by a bronze statue of George Washington, the inscription carved across the top of the monument reads, "Freedom is a light for which many men have died in darkness." A few blocks away, on the grounds of the Pennsylvania Hospital, is the Physic Garden where some of the herbal cures used by physicians of the colonial period are grown.

FRANKLIN SQUARE

Franklin Square, between Race and Vine and 6th and 7th Streets in the northeast quadrant, forms the entrance to the Franklin Bridge, dedicated in 1926 and linking Philadelphia and Camden, New Jersey. The lquare is punctuated by Isamu Noguchi's stainless-steel sculpture of a kite, key and lightning bolt, unmistakable symbols of Philadelphia's resident genius, Benjamin Franklin. People are familiar with Franklin's experiments with electricity, but relatively few know of his relentless efforts to introduce plants and improve agricultural practices. These and many other Franklin stories are told at Franklin Court on Orianna Street between 3rd and 4th and at Bartram's Garden.

RITTENHOUSE SQUARE

Rittenhouse Square is one of the most intensively utilized parks in Philadelphia and also one of the most fashionable addresses. It is bounded by 18th and 19th and Locust Streets forming the southwest quadrant of the grid. Commemorating David Rittenhouse (1732–1796), colonial scientist, philosopher and printer, the area was once the hunting ground of the rich. The present form of the Square, with fountains and statuary are the work of Paul Philippe Cret, one of the designers of the Benjamin Franklin Parkway and architect of Albert Barnes's art gallery. A Philadelphia tradition since 1914, the Flower Mart is held in Rittenhouse Square every May to raise money for hospitals.

LOGAN CIRCLE
Logan Circle is the hub of the Benjamin Franklin Parkway. It started, as did the others, as a square; its geometry was reshaped, however, after the turn of the century when the Parkway was created. The circle of handsome Princess trees (*Paulownia tomentosa*) and colorful spring bulbs grace the restored Swann Fountain, a garden highlight maintained by area businesses and museums. It commemorates James Logan (1674–1751), William Penn's agent and another of Philadelphia's Renaissance men who contributed much to the early gardening traditions.

BENJAMIN FRANKLIN PARKWAY
Two hundred and thirty-five years after Captain Thomas Holmes set forth his formula for ordered growth, a 250-foot corridor, approximately one mile long, was cut to the very heart of the city. Many of this country's most important museums with their classical architecture fortify the Parkway. The Philadelphia Museum of Art occupies a site that William Penn referred to as his Faire Mount. It was a trek out

of the city to this site in the late 18th and much of the 19th century; but then that is what William Penn had in mind for his city.

The Rodin Museum, under the direction of the Philadelphia Museum of Art, is located a little down from the Art Museum along the Parkway. The Franklin Institute, Academy of Natural Science and Free Library rim Logan Circle with art, science and learning, to make this one of the country's major hubs of history and education.

Jacques Greber (1882–1962) is the landscape designer who brought the park into the city and in so doing created the ambiance for many of Philadelphia's festivals held each year on the Parkway. The original wedge-shaped form of Greber's design remains intact, although many of the trees have had to be replaced. The single species plantings of sycamore are giving way to mixed plantings of oak, maple and sweet gum, reflecting current trends in ecological thinking—unity of design in plantings yielding to a mixture in an effort to achieve biological stability.

THE SCHUYLKILL RIVER
The Schuylkill River had long been a corridor for trade as well as the major escape route for those who could afford a second home in the country. With its boats of all description, green forests and steep banks it offered a picturesque subject for painters who chronicled this culture's changing views of nature. The Fairmount Waterworks also provided opportunities to harness nature with state-of-the-art technology to solve one of the fundamental problems of the city, the quest for a healthy and adequate supply of water. By 1819 the decision was made to abandon steam power in

Sculler on the Schuylkill River

favor of more reliable and cheaper water power. The first water went over the dam in 1821 and a year later the water wheels became the propulsion to push the water up into the reservoir.

In his mill house, Frederick Graff (1774–1847) returned to the architectural style of his mentor, Benjamin Henry Latrobe (1764–1820) and designed the neoclassical temple-like structures on either end of the 238-foot mill house. By 1835 an elaborate garden had grown up around this engineering marvel to proclaim that a cultured city could solve a fundamental problem in ways that would both delight the eye and inform the public, bringing praise and even international acclaim to Philadelphia. The Waterworks became a necessary stop on everyone's visit to the city, including Mark

Twain, who wrote in a letter of 1853 to his brother in Hannibal, "Unlike New York, I like this Phila amazingly, and the people in it. . . ."

As hydraulic technology advanced, the city became less dependent upon Fairmount Waterworks, and by the 1880s the site began to deteriorate. In 1911 it was decommissioned as a pumping station. But it still had a role to play. On this site the forest was cleared to make way for a reservoir to quench a city's thirst, the reservoir was later converted to educational purposes as an aquarium and finally the aquarium was rebaptized for recreational purposes as an olympic swimming pool. In its last incarnation, William Penn's Faire Mount becomes the foundation for a temple to the muses.

Swann Fountain at Logan Square

EAST PARK

LEMON HILL

Lemon Hill is part of William Penn's Spring-ettsbury Manor, where the founder instructed that grapes be planted in hopes of establishing a wine industry. (It was unsuccessful.) The property was purchased and named "The Hills" by Robert Morris, the major financier of the Revolutionary War, whose monetary wizardry kept the Yorktown Campaign going and resulted in the defeat of Cornwallis. He was a signer of the Declaration of Independence and adviser and friend of George Washington. Morris built a stately summer home here in 1770, a venue for lavish entertaining of guests, including the Washingtons. The house was burned by the British and rebuilt by Morris after the war. Bad real estate investments after the war, however, brought Morris's financial empire tumbling down. An advocate of prison for debtors, Robert Morris himself spent four years in debtors' prison on Walnut Street, where he once again entertained George Washington. He died a broken man.

"The Hills," which had burned down a second time in 1781, was purchased by Henry Pratt in 1799. He built the present house and developed an elaborate garden that became a national showplace. Pratt named his estate Lemon Hill for the lemons he found growing in Morris's great greenhouses when he bought the property. It was purchased by the City in 1844 and was part of the original acreage that created Fairmount Park when it officially came into existence in 1855.

MOUNT PLEASANT

Mount Pleasant, an outstanding example of Georgian architecture with a superb Palladian window, was built in 1761 by a Scottish sea captain, John McPherson, who made his money as a privateer, a job that cost him an arm. McPherson helped organize the patriot's navy and lost John Jr. at the battle of Quebec. William, his other son, was commissioned a Brigadier General by President Adams and served as a delegate to the Pennsylvania Convention to ratify the Constitution. In 1779 the house was purchased by Benedict Arnold as a

wedding present for his wife, but thanks to his misguided career moves, it was never used.

All we know of McPherson's garden is that he had a large walled vegetable garden, in the Scottish tradition, fruit orchards and meadows. At the time of the Sesquicentennial a grand Colonial Revival garden was created on the riverside, the sad remnants of which are all that is now visible.

STRAWBERRY MANSION

The Hood family built a house on the site in 1768, and Robin Hood Dell is where the summer concerts of the Philadelphia Orchestra are performed. Charles Thomson (1729–1824), Irish-born teacher of language at Franklin Academy, merchant and permanent secretary of the Continental Congress, lived in the Hood house during the time of the Revolutionary War. Like Lemon Hill, the house was burned by the British when they were searching for official papers. In 1798 another house, Somerton, was built on this site and owned by Judge William Lewis, a Quaker and friend of Washington and Hamilton, who wrote some of the first antislavery laws.

The Hemphills were the next to occupy these grounds and Coleman, son of Judge Joseph Hemphill, seems to have been at least partially responsible for the name, Strawberry Mansion, in that their son imported strawberries from Chile. According to the late John F. Marion, however, the name dates from the 1840s when a Mrs. Grimes sold strawberries and cream there. Coleman Hemphill is also reported to have been responsible for the mansion's south wing ballroom, added in 1825 when his parents were in Europe. When the

Judge returned he added the north wing a few years later.

Strawberry Mansion, furnished in the Empire style, has one of the more colorful histories of the Park houses. It was also a beer garden, a resort featuring Italian cuisine, brothel, police court and a recreation area for park guards. And if legend has it correct, at one time there was a speakeasy in the cellar.

Laurel Hill

Laurel Hill, a fine example of Georgian architecture and so named because of the abundant mountain laurel in this area, was built by Joseph Shute in 1748. The property was purchased in 1760 by a wealthy and cultured Philadelphia gentleman, Francis Rawle and his wife Rebecca. After her husband was killed in a hunting accident, Rebecca married Samuel Shoemaker, who had occupied many important posts under the British government and was a loyalist during the Revolutionary War. He left the city when the British departed, and the house was confiscated. Rebecca Rawle Shoemaker managed to regain possession, and lived at Laurel Hill until her death, when it was sold to Dr. Philip Syng (1768–1837), who purchased it as a wedding present to his daughter Mrs. Jacob Randolph, after which it became known as the Randolph Mansion.

Ormiston

Ormiston was built by Joseph Galloway sometime before the Revolutionary War and named for the family seat in Edinburgh. Galloway, Benjamin Franklin's political partner before they parted company, was a successful Philadelphia lawyer who married well and served as speaker of the Assembly from 1765 to 1777. He also served as Provost Marshal during the British occupation and was rewarded for his loyalty to the British Crown by having Ormiston confiscated. Galloway fled to Bucks County and later to England with Lord Howe; he died there in 1803. By 1799 Ormiston had been bought by Edward Burd, and the grounds were laid out with a variety of fruit trees.

Woodford

Woodford began as a one-story farmhouse located near a ford in the woods, and along the major thoroughfare between Philadelphia and Norristown. The first floor dates to 1756 and the second to 1772. William Coleman, a much-respected friend of Benjamin Franklin and holder of many important city posts, remodeled the existing structure in 1756. Coleman died without issue and left Woodford to his nephew, who later sold it to Alexander Barclay, His Majesty's Comptroller of Customs. After Barclay's death in 1771 it became the home of Mrs. Barclay's sister, the wife of a wealthy Jewish merchant, David Frank, who also served as a Crown Agent in Philadelphia. He added the second floor including the Palladian window. During the occupation, Woodford was one of the social centers for British officers and a frequent destination for Lord Howe. These loyalist activities aroused a tide of resentment after the war, and David Frank was arrested twice for providing information to the enemy. He was acquitted, but in 1780 the Franks departed for New York and Woodford was confiscated.

Laurel Hill Cemetery

LAUREL HILL CEMETERY

This site, once the home of Joseph Sims, became a cemetery in 1837. The curving paths, sculpture, memorials and varieties of trees, laid out by John Notman (1810–1865), choreographed the movements of an urban population seeking to escape life in the city, and under its dramatically high ground above the Schuylkill River lie many of the great Philadelphians who created the modern city. Laurel Hill, like Mount Auburn in Boston and Greenwood in Brooklyn, was a forerunner of the great urban parks which appeared under the guidance of Olmsted and Vaux, in the second half of the 19th century.

WEST PARK

THE SOLITUDE
John Penn (1760–1834), grandson of William Penn, built The Solitude in 1785. A graduate of Cambridge University and a poet, he created the first Robert Adam-style house in America.

Azalea garden in Fairmount Park

He designed a perfect English landscape as a setting for his elegant house, with a bowling green, vistas created through the woods, a wilderness, and flower and vegetable gardens tucked out of sight. His ha-ha kept his deer herd in bounds (portent of today's problem). The Solitude is now the administrative offices of the Philadelphia Zoological Society.

SWEETBRIAR

Sweetbriar was the home of another prominent Philadelphia citizen, Samuel Breck (1771–1862). Schooled in France, friend of the Marquis de Lafayette, devotee of the arts, Breck was a political as well as a social power; in 1834 he obtained a statewide, tax-supported system of schools. The property was a wedding gift from his father-in-law, John Ross. He built Sweetbriar to his own refined tastes, with lawns, woods, gardens and greenhouses.

LETITIA STREET HOUSE

Two houses were moved into the West Park from other parts of the city to enshrine the city's interest in its architectural history and the Park as a suitable repository for that history. The house, so named for its original site on Letitia Street, which ran from Front to 2nd Street, was built some time between 1703 and 1715 by John Smart, a carpenter. A fine example of early 18th century row-house architecture with Queen Anne furnishings, it was moved to Fairmount in 1883.

CEDAR GROVE

Cedar Grove was constructed in 1721 in Harrowgate near Frankfort, a Quaker resort with mineral springs. It was dismantled and re-assembled in Fairmount Park in 1927 at the expense of Lydia T. Morris, co-founder with her brother of the Morris Arboretum of the University of Pennsylvania. The object was to have on display the early Quaker lifestyle. Inside the white picket fence is an herb garden maintained by the Philadelphia Unit of the Herb Society of America.

GREENLAND

Greenland started as a substantial farmhouse about 1825 and was modified over the years before it came into the hands of Joshua B. Lippincott, founder of J. B. Lippincott and Company. It was sold to the City in 1869.

THE LILACS

The Lilacs, named for the lilac bushes which surrounded it, was started as an 18th century farmhouse, to which a contrasting addition in the Federal style was made in 1832. Later owned by the University Barge Club, it was the destination for gentlemen boaters and their lady friends.

CHAMOUNIX MANSION

Chamounix Mansion was built by George Plumstead in 1800 in the Federal style of architecture. The gardens have been described as being of a formal boxwood design with trees planted to honor the nation's leaders: black walnut for Robert Morris, American chestnut for Thomas Jefferson and the Tulip tree for George Washington.

BELMONT MANSION

Partially hidden by 19th century additions—including a third floor—Belmont Mansion has been under-appreciated until recently. The property, with its magnificent vista of Philadelphia, was purchased in 1742 by the loyalist Judge William Peters, who built the mansion and created an elaborate garden, with an allee of cherry trees toward the river, and a formal garden with statuary and a maze. It later passed to his son Richard (1744–1828), an ardent supporter of Independence and friend of Washington, Madison and Benjamin Franklin. Richard Peters was a founder of the Philadelphia Society for the Promotion of Agriculture, and under his tenure, Belmont became a model farm. The house deteriorated in the late 19th century, but is now being restored to its 18th century grandeur by the Fairmount Park Commission together with the Fairmount Park Historic Preservation Trust, Inc.

RIDGELAND

Ridgeland was another farmhouse dating to the late 18th century, and onetime residence of the Director of Fairmount Park.

OHIO HOUSE

Ohio House was one of only two structures remaining from the Centennial Exhibition, the other being Memorial Hall. It was recently renovated for the administrative offices of the Park Ranger Corps.

THE CENTENNIAL EXHIBITION

Horticulture Hall, designed by Herman J. Schwartzmann for the Centennial Exhibition, was a grand building 383 feet long, 192 feet wide and 69 feet tall, and designed as one of the few buildings to remain after the Exhibition closed. It stood until 1955, when it was demolished. On this site the Plant and Garden Center of Fairmount Park was erected in 1977–1979. Only in the Pennsylvania Horticulture Society's Fall shows, which are now held here, can we hear the faint echo of what it was like when Horticulture Hall was filled with plants and flowers during the Centennial celebrations.

Twenty-six of the 37 states and territories and 56 foreign countries were represented in the Centennial Exhibition. The horticultural exhibits represented all kinds of styles, including the Japanese, which had not been seen before in this country on any kind of scale. The opportunity to bring back this style of gardening to Fairmount Park came about through the St. Louis World's Fair, where the Japanese Temple Gate was purchased and brought back to Philadelphia in 1905 by John H. Converse and Samuel Vauclain. The design of the gardens surrounding the gate were by Y. Muto, designer of the Japanese-style gardens of the Morris Arboretum, and were donated by John T. Morris and John Converse. Unfortunately the gate burned to the ground on May 6, 1955.

The precedent of a Japanese garden planted on this site was sufficient to cause the present house to be moved here in 1957. The authentic Japanese house is designed by prominent Japanese architect, Junzo Yoshimura, based

Japanese Garden in Fairmount Park

upon 17th century designs. With seeds first planted in the Centennial Exhibition it was presented by the American-Japan Society of Tokyo, and is one of the most complete and authentic Japanese gardens in the area. Today it is maintained by the Friends of the Japanese Garden, who include in their programs Japanese tea ceremonies.

THE ACT OF CONSOLIDATION, 1854

To further the ideals of the "greene Country Towne" in the mid-18th century, Philadelphia needed more land to be annexed to the city. On February 2, 1854, the Act of Consolidation created new city limits, dissected by a much longer stretch of the Schuylkill to the north and south and new sections of the Wissahickon, Tacony and Pennypack streams and their tributaries.

A seven-mile stretch of the Wissahickon Creek was part of this annexation. The stream courses through an ancient rock formation and the valley was originally clothed in a rich mix of oak, chestnut and hickory. The Lenni Lenape once called this home and named the stream for the abundant catfish (wisamickaw) or yellow color (wisauchsickaw)—either description would apply. A memorial above Valley Green in the form of a statue of an Indian scout commemorates their having passed this way. The tributary of the Schuylkill has one of the richest histories of any stream in the country and was celebrated by Edgar Allan Poe in an article of 1843. It became a part of Fairmount Park in 1867 and was placed on the National Register of Natural Historic Landmarks in 1972.

The machine came early to the Wissahickon Valley. The fall rate of the stream was sufficient to provide the energy to turn many wheels of the new industrial city. Robeson's Sawmill at the mouth of the Wissahickon was on stream in 1683 and mills continued to be built through the 18th century. Many of these operated well into the 1860s. The Rittenhouse Mills and birthplace of David Rittenhouse were started in 1869 by William Rittenhouse, Sr., who established the first paper mill in this country. Rittenhouse Village is one of the last reminders of the time when water powered Philadelphia to make it the industrial center of the emerging nation. These mills were acquired by the Fairmount Park Commission in the 1870s.

"To be laid out and maintained forever as an open public place and park, for the health and enjoyment of the people of the said City, and the preservation of the water supply" ACT OF THE GENERAL ASSEMBLY, MARCH 26, 1867

The Andorra Nature Center is located off Forbidden Drive, the last outpost of the Wissahickon. Grasshopper sparrows, Acadian flycatchers and cerulean warblers make their way through ancient white oaks and tulip trees in these woods. It is here where the staccato tapping of the pileated woodpecker can now and then be heard telegraphing a message of van-

ishing wilderness. The Center was founded in 1978, a response to the Bicentennial call.

After the turn of this century, the Park Commission moved to protect other stream corridors, including Cobbs Creek and the Pennypack. The Pennypack has been a focus of environmental interest paralleling the Wissahickon, and in 1978 the Pennypack Environ-

Stairway to the Wissahickon

Wissahickon tributary

mental Center was founded. Carpenter's Woods, a tributary of the Wissahickon and temporary home for Hooded Warblers, was added in 1916, and the Pocquessing Creek in the 1960s.

From the beginning, urban parks, seen as promoting public health and recreational pursuits, were part of the park's mandate. In 1870 land was acquired for the Walnut Lane golf course. Five other golf courses were located throughout the city to accommodate the growing popularity of the sport: Juanita (1915), Cobbs Creek (1920), Karakung (1920), Roosevelt Park (1922) and John Byrne (1972). The 19th century park as pleasure ground for passive recreation and enjoyment of open space or retreat from city squalor would give way in the 20th century to park as playground.

The period from 1910 to 1930 was one of active land acquisition as the Commission proceeded to acquire land for neighborhood parks. These vary in size and shape from the one-acre square Palmer Park in an intensively developed neighborhood in Kensington to the more than 300-acre Franklin D. Roosevelt Park and golf course off Broad Street in South Philadelphia that was designed by Olmsted's firm.

The functions of these neighborhood parks vary as much as their size. Pastorius Park in the affluent Chestnut Hill section of the city is in the tradition of the pleasure grounds of the past with concerts and Shakespearean drama in the summer and ice-skating in the winter. Far Country in West Mount Airy is being developed into the mayor's residence, whereas before it was an arboretum and bird sanctuary.

In the north there is Awbury Park, Fernhill, Fisher Park, Hunting Park and Wakefield Park; in the south, Marconi Plaza and Franklin D. Roosevelt; in the northeast Burholm (Fox Chase) and Eden Hall; and in the west, Morris Park and Carroll Park. In Center City Schuylkill River Park was added in 1966. All are centers of community activity with playing fields and in several cases recreational centers for indoor sports and community meetings.

As the automobile came to dominate life in the city, the beautification of motorways came to take a leading place on the Park Commission's agenda. Two hundred and fifty acres along a 12-mile stretch of Roosevelt Boulevard was incorporated into Fairmount Park in 1916. The Cobbs Creek Parkway runs for almost four miles, and a 23-acre section of Southern Boulevard was added in 1923.

The Benjamin Franklin Parkway, installed between 1915 and 1928, was to show that these motorways could be functional as well as beautiful. Kelly Drive (East Park) and the West Park Drives were to show that they could be picturesque. The Schuylkill Expressway, completed in 1959, was to demonstrate that the value of moving masses of people from place to place exceeded the values attached to its park.

To manage the city's park system which is spread over about 9000 acres and includes 375 buildings, there are fewer than 400 full-time park employees and an annual operating budget of around $12 million—somewhat less than the operating budget of Longwood Gardens.

Stone bridge crossing the Wissahickon

A symbol of our progress in relations with the animal kingdom—from animal houses to habitats to preserves

Zoological Society of Philadelphia

The Peacable Kingdom

Author JOHN SEDGWICK
on the Philadelphia Zoo

THE PHILADELPHIA ZOO is located at the south end of the West Park section of Fairmount Park. The gatehouses, designed by Frank Furness, were constructed in 1876, two years after the Zoo opened its gates to the public July 1, 1874. Wilhelm Wolff's sculpture, Dying Lioness, at the entrance, symbolizing man's painful relationship with animals, sets the stage for this drama; it first appeared at the Centennial Exhibition.

The Philadelphia Zoo itself is a symbol of our progress in relations with the animal world—from Animal Houses, to Habitats, and finally to Preserve. Woven through these exhibitions is a fourth dimension, the human stage or animal mall made up of walks, picnic areas and gazeboes. The Rare Animal House, Small Mammal House, Reptile House, Pachyderm House and Carnivore House, lining the wide walkway that gently arcs south and westward, bear testimony to a time when the Philadelphia Zoo saw itself as a kind of housing development for exotic animals. Nineteenth century zoos were animal menageries built to satisfy a public's curiosity that was being aroused as the more remote parts of the world became accessible through travel.

World of Primates (1986), Bird Valley (1954), Bear Country (1980), African Plains I and II (1974 and 1976) and the most recent Carnivore Kingdom (1992) reflect more recent trends in exhibiting animals. They are placed in settings contrived to resemble or simulate native habitats. A few hardy bamboos and the tree of heaven help to give a sense of lushness of tropical climes, and pampas grass and locust trees help conjure up the African plains.

"And of every living thing of all flesh, two of every sort shall thou bring into the ark, to keep them alive with thee; they shall be male and female." GENESIS 6:19

Through the rest of the exhibits, stately trees are dispersed as single specimens or in groves to form the backbone of the plant collection and lend credibility to the often-repeated claim that this is indeed a zoological garden. As in the case of the animals, these trees are of both native and exotic origin: the specimen ginkgo near the impala fountain, Kwanzan cherries and London planes all hail from distant shores, while the pin oaks, black oaks, elms and yellowwood are a gathering from America's forests. There are 208 species of trees in the Zoo's collection, including an American elm planted during the 1876 Centennial and an English elm planted about 1787 by William Penn's grandson, John. Contrast this with about 550 species of animals represented by approximately 1,700 specimens. The ratio reminds us that the known world's fauna outnumbers the world's flora in species by about 30:1, if we include insects in these numbers.

The Bird House located near the center of the Zoo is another example of the evolution of the relationship between plants and animals. Built in 1916, it was a house of cages for birds. Remodeled in the 1950s and again in 1987, in its most recent incarnation the birds are allowed to fly freely amid a housescape of tropical plants.

Penn's Woodland Trail at the south end of the Zoo was installed in 1982 in celebration of the Tercentenary of the founding of Philadelphia. A short serpentine path runs through the exhibition with areas on either side planted with a mixture of native trees, hemlock, holly, cedar and honey locust, and shrubs, winterberry and mountain laurel. Near the entrance there is a cattail marsh. Water spouts from a bare pipe protruding at the edge, and surrounding this basin is a low fence. In this woodsy setting more animals, such as bobcats, porcupines and grouse, are presented in wire cages scattered among the trees, a throwback to earlier times.

Chartered in 1859 as the Philadelphia Zoological Society, the Garden has leased this 42-acre parcel of ground from the Fairmount Park Commission since 1872. It is one of the city's most popular attractions, and has one of the largest support groups of any of Philadelphia's museums.

The college campus as community park

The American College Arboretum

Beauty in the environment—art, horticulture and architecture—is a positive motivating force for achievement in education.

THE AMERICAN COLLEGE philosophy

THE 45-ACRE campus arboretum of The American College is located in Bryn Mawr approximately 12 miles northwest of Philadelphia. It is a private, independent, non-traditional, accredited college founded in 1927 by S. S. Huebner. The entire campus has been developed as a landscape amenity, or better yet, an outdoor classroom, with a labeled collection of trees and shrubs that give it the character of an arboretum, while the openness of the institution to the surrounding community with its jogging paths has promoted the use of the space as a public park and recreation area.

Entering the campus off Bryn Mawr Avenue, specimen trees of pignut hickory (*Carya glabra*), white oak (*Quercus alba*), scarlet oak (*Quercus coccinea*) and American beech (*Fagus grandifolia*) tell us that we have entered a place that cares about its trees. There are 28 specimen trees identified throughout the campus; some of these date back to the late 19th century when the property belonged to Stanley Flagg. Mr. Flagg had hired a young horticulturalist by the name of Harry Wood to assist him in his planting. When The American College first started acquiring the property in 1959, Harry Wood came back to save some of these specimens he had helped plant.

The tradition of promoting trees has continued to be encouraged with the planting of class trees and the practice of dedicating trees in honor or memory of those who have been associated with the College. An English oak (*Quercus robur*) adds another growth ring each year to honor the memory of Harry Wood.

Other garden features have been added over the years to enhance the landscape and reflect the current concerns over preservation.

In the English tradition of landscape architect Lancelot "Capability" Brown, a dam and lake were constructed in 1968 to serve as a focal point. The Boettner Woodland Garden, created by William Terrence McDonnell, the College's horticulturalist, covers an area of approximately 10 acres and is being developed for year-round color and garden interest and the ever-widening enthusiasm for woodland gardening.

Up until 1961 The American College was on the University of Pennsylvania campus. It has a faculty of 40 and offers correspondence courses in financial management to 45,000 students scattered around the world.

A business school that has discovered that one of the best insurance policies may be written in terms of a partnership with nature

259

"From western lands beyond the foam / We sought our English father's home."   MARY S. COPE, 1886

Awbury Arboretum

I'm very impressed with the trees here in Awbury. They are lovely big specimens. . . . What I want to see is trees which really look as if they are enjoying themselves.

Sir Peter Shepheard, 1988

The Awbury Arboretum covers an area of 55 acres in the Germantown/Mount Airy sections of Philadelphia. The old Pennsylvania Railroad runs along the western border with the Washington Lane station providing convenient public transportation to this urban park and living legacy of one of Philadelphia's prominent Quaker families.

The original design of this park can be easily read at the Washington Lane station entrance: a series of open meadows walled off on the edges and along the gently curving corridors by mature specimens of oak, tulip poplar, sycamore, beech, ash, hickory and maple. Along the southern boundary there is a screening planting of conifers, Austrian pine, Douglas fir, arbor vitae and white pine. Character-laden trees "enjoying themselves" can be found throughout the park.

The pond to the north of the Washington Lane station entrance was excavated shortly after Awbury was officially designated an arboretum in 1918. It was restored in the early 1980s with city funds for urban redevelopment. An area of approximately 20 acres on the north side of Washington Lane was designated as a nature preserve in 1985. The community gardens at the northeast limit of the property, where neighborhood families grow their own vegetables, were established in the early 1970s. They are the most recent response to the needs that can be met by our urban open spaces.

Through all the changes which have taken place on this property over the years, the Awbury Arboretum is still a reflection of the English style of landscape gardening that came into vogue in the 17th century and was widely promoted in this country throughout the 18th and 19th centuries. The name Awbury comes from Avebury, England, the ancestral home of Oliver Cope, who purchased land in 1681 from William Penn and settled his family in Pennsylvania.

Thomas Pym Cope (1768–1854), founder of the Cope packet line that sailed between Philadelphia and Liverpool, created the wealth and established the family as one of Philadelphia's leading mercantile powers. The family fortunes were continued by his sons, one of whom, Henry (1793–1865), purchased 40 acres in east Germantown in 1852 from the actress Charlotte Cushman and started to build his summer home the following year. Henry's son Thomas (1823–1900) had visited English parks and gardens as a young man and is credited as the one most responsible for the landscape design. The work of a well-known Scots landscape designer, William Saunders, who trained at the Royal Botanic Garden, Kew, and

Thomas W. Sears, another prominent landscaper working in this region in the 1930s, also contributed to the design of the property.

The Francis Cope House was built in 1862 by Henry Cope for his elder son Francis R. Cope (1821–1909), who followed in his father's footsteps as a man of public affairs. With its Gothic architecture dramatically sited on top of a rise, it forms the centerpiece of this landscape. On a clear day, one can see the city of Philadelphia from the porch. The Cope House serves as the base of operations for the Awbury Arboretum Assocation, an organization founded in 1985 to manage the property and oversee educational programs. In 1916 20 acres of the family estate was deeded by Annette Cope to the City Parks Association, a not-for-profit agency established in 1888 to promote parks and recreation. Her sister Caroline Cope, who died in 1944 at the age of 104, left trust funds to purchase other lands and manage the property.

OPPOSITE: *To see where our urban parks are going the Awbury Arboretum is the place to look*

The Quaker founders felt strongly that education for women could change society for the better—"refinement of heart, mind and manners"

Bryn Mawr College

A democratic village around the green
... representing the whole life possible in
a fully integrated society.

GEORGE THOMAS, architectural historian

THE 112-ACRE campus is located in the suburbs of Bryn Mawr, approximately 11 miles west of Philadelphia. The preferred entrance to this collegiate campus built for Quaker daughters is off Merion Avenue, passing through the heraldic lions honoring past president Mary Catherine McBride (1942–1970), and through the Pembroke Hall arch, the 1894 masterwork of Philadelphia architects Walter Cope and John Stewardson. The oak-lined walk beyond the arch is bracketed by Taylor Hall, named after the College's founder, with its impressive Gothic tower, the 1879 work of Addison Hutton, the College's first architect, and the Martha Carey Thomas Library, designed by Stewardson and Cope and constructed in 1906, four years after the death of Walter Cope at the age of 42.

The paved walk terminates in a grass-lined double row of Oak trees, Senior Row. Scattered throughout the campus are many fine old specimen trees: basswood (*Tilia petiolarus*), American ash (*Fraxinus americana*) and sassafras (*Sassafras albidum*), moving this park into the direction of a campus arboretum. If the impression one receives upon entering this courtyard is one of having arrived on the campus of an Oxford or Cambridge college, then the desired effect has been achieved.

In June of 1895, Frederick Law Olmsted, in failing health, visited the Bryn Mawr College campus at the request of Martha Carey Thomas, the College's second president. The pattern of placement of buildings on the campus had already been established, but an unambiguous entrance was lacking. Olmsted proposed the axial treatment through the arches at Pembroke, extending beyond Taylor

Hall and then cutting diagonally to the northwest and opening out onto the playing fields.

Bryn Mawr administrators were determined to have the Quaker daughters strong in both body and mind, and plenty of attention was given to the location of the playing fields. This problem was certainly not something new for Olmsted; he had dealt with it many times in Central Park. The solution he chose was to place the playing fields down on the bottom of the slope, surround them by a running track and screen them from view. Embracing the entire design was a carriage road that he urged the administration to build, although sadly his advice was never followed.

The Bryn Mawr College campus reflects the attitude of how landscape and architecture ultimately impress themselves upon growing minds and established values. The conscious intent to adopt an architectural style that would lift young women in their educational surroundings out of the present and back in space and time was a novel idea. Moreover, a women's college campus with its strongly masculine architecture must have represented a particularly interesting problem for Olmsted. His solutions in this, one of his last works, survive as testaments to his skill and the imagination of those who followed. In 1991 the Bryn Mawr College campus was placed on the National Register of Historic Buildings in recognition of the importance of buildings and landscape.

The cradle of collegiate architecture in an Olmstedian landscape

The garden as artifact of nature and stage upon which the human drama is performed

Independence National Historical Park

*Let every House be placed if the Person pleases
in the middle of its platt as to the breadthway of
it, that so there may be ground on each side, for
Gardens or Orchards or fields, that it may be a
greene Country Towne, which will never
be burn't and always be wholesome.*

WILLIAM PENN, 1681

THE STORY of this nation's founding is framed in Philadelphia by Race Street on the north, Walnut on the south, Second on the East and Sixth on the West. Within this area, Independence National Historical Park, signed into law by President Harry Truman in 1948, includes 42 acres and encompasses 40 of this nation's most historic buildings. It is here where the story of William Penn's "holy experiment" had its beginnings in 1682: religious freedom giving rise to a secular society and individual freedom institutionalized into a republican form of government.

Welcome Park provides the map for Penn's holy quest. *Welcome* was the name of Penn's ship that landed to the south of present-day Philadelphia on October 7, 1682. The grid laid out by Thomas Holmes, William Penn's surveyor, reveals a design for ordered growth, with Market Street (High Street in the original) extending in an east-west direction from the Delaware to the Schuylkill and Broad Street, a north-south axis, intersecting Market about midway between the two rivers.

In this walled model of Philadelphia the Proprietor stands at Center Square, where City Hall is now located, hand outstretched in a gesture of a peaceful lawgiver. The four planters, each with a single Callery pear, underscore Penn's intentions to make this a "greene Country Towne." They symbolize the four squares, Washington, Rittenhouse, Franklin and Logan.

The Slate Roof House, the address of William Penn from 1699 to 1701, once stood on the site now occupied by Welcome Park. Close by were the oaks, hickories and tulip trees that made up much of the dense forests

Views of equality, unalienable rights and the pursuit of happiness were to lead to a standard of living that the world had never before known

of Penn's woods. It was here where William Penn's divinely-inspired community was to first take root.

Dispute over land and self-determination arose early between the colonists and the proprietor. In an effort to appease the landed Quaker elite, on October 28, 1701, before he left his beloved Pennsylvania for the last time, Penn granted the Charter of Privileges and raised the "greene Country Towne" to the status of a city.

Across the street from the Slate Roof House of William Penn was City Tavern. The original, built in 1773, became the center of social and political activity, mostly focused on increasingly difficult relations between the colonists and the mother country. Here Paul Revere came in 1774 with news of the closing of the port of Boston, and later that year the First Continental Congress was formed while the founders of this nation shuttled between City Tavern and Carpenter's Hall, informally and formally exploring their options. Many of the issues concerned land. As Thomas Jefferson instructed his delegates to the Congress in 1774, "We shall at this time also take notice of an error in the nature of our landholdings, which crept in at a very early period of our settlement. . . . Our ancestors who immigrated hither were farmers, not lawyers."

Behind City Tavern is a Federal period style garden constructed as a memorial to Stephen Girard, banker and philanthropist. The gently curving herringbone brickwork of the path and informal planting of the beds represent a departure from the tight forms of the parterred gardens of the earlier 18th century.

Three gardens, also representing variations on the 18th century theme, are entered from the alley to the north of Walnut between 3rd and 4th Streets. Bishop White's Garden at the corner of Walnut and 3rd, with its stately willow oaks, holly and boxwood hedges, fountains and benches, is a cool garden for contemplation. Close by are the gardens of two of Philadelphia's most prominent citizens, Dr. Benjamin Rush and Dolley Todd Madison. The ordered spaces of the parterred garden would have suited the mind of Dr. Rush, a man of the Enlightenment, whose house stood at the corner of Walnut and 3rd Streets. Dolley Todd lived with her lawyer husband, John, a block away on Walnut and 4th. John died in the yellow fever epidemic of 1793, and a year later Dolley married James Madison. Behind the Todd house (built in 1775) is another colonial kitchen garden, its carrots, beets, onions and corn reminding us that first and foremost these gardens were planted to provide the necessities of life.

The London plane trees (*Platanus x acerifolia*), with their broad leaves and shredding bark lining many of these streets, are hybrid introductions, the progeny of an accidental cross between an American sycamore (*Platanus occidentalis*) and an Asian sycamore (*Platanus orientalis*). The willow (*Salix babylonica*) behind Bishop White's house (which was built in 1786–1787) is likewise an introduction as well as a reminder of Benjamin Franklin's notable contributions to diversifying the garden flora. Even the weeds that grow between the cobble-paved Dock Street, goose grass (*Eleusina indica*), groundsel (*Senecio vulgaris*) and annual bluegrass (*Poa annua*), might well be the progeny of seed carried with the packing materials that brought our forefathers and mothers to this country.

Behind and to the west of the Pennsylvania Horticultural Society headquarters are examples of colonial style gardens. While the design may be inspired by that period, in the choice of plants and arrangement they clearly reflect 20th century tastes and preferences. The garden to the south of Walnut between 4th and 5th Streets features roses and tells of our long-standing love affair with that notorious genus which, after years of debate, became the national flower. A gift from the Daughters of the American Revolution, the Rose Garden was dedicated in 1971 in memory of the signers of the Declaration of Independence. To the south of Locust between 4th and 5th Streets is the Magnolia Garden. This garden was originally planned as a gathering of representatives from each of the 48 states. It was dedicated in 1959 by the Garden Club of America to the Founders of America.

The 18th century landscape of Independence Square, where on July 8, 1776, the Declaration of Independence was read aloud, was designed by Samuel Vaughan, an Englishman. The present landscape dates to 1915–1916 when a mid-19th century courthouse that stood on this site was removed. Instead of returning to the original landscape, the planners yielded to an early 20th century design, maintaining more open access to the neighborhood.

To the south and west of Independence Square is Washington Square, one of the four originals in William Penn's grand design to create a "greene Country Towne." Under the high canopy of sycamore, locust, catalpa, basswood and ginkgo, lie the remains of Conti-nental soldiers and British prisoners, casualties of deeds done and undone in transforming Penn's holy experiment into an experiment in self-government.

To the north of Market, Independence Mall continues with the large rectangular paved spaces, bracketed by oak (*Quercus suba*), and punctuated by a fountain, a memorial to Judge Edwin O. Lewis, who admired the spacious boulevards of Paris and helped inspire the City Beautiful movement that gave us the Benjamin Franklin Parkway.

On Market between 3rd and 4th, the 18th century streetscape marks the entrance to Franklin Court, home of Philadelphia's most famous citizen, Benjamin Franklin (1706–1790). He built his house between 1763 and 1765, and from his letters to his sister we learn how his garden evolved. "Considering our well-furnished plentiful market as the best of gardens, I am turning mine, in the midst of which my house stands, into grass plots and gravel walks, with trees and flowering shrubs."

Today, the garden with its single mulberry tree, planters of the Chinese scholar's tree and a steel frame ghosting the space where his house once stood, are the abstract representatives of this 18th century landscape. The treatment of the garden and building, designed by Philadelphia architect Robert Venturi, represented a landmark in historic preservation when it was opened to the public in 1975. Instead of trying to recreate a picture of the past, the National Park Service chose instead to expose archeological digs and treat the garden and house symbolically. It was a radical departure from the widely-acclaimed Williamsburg approach that had been so influential in set-

The Holy Experiment set in motion a series of changes which not only altered the political climate of the world forever but the global climate as well

ting the course for Independence Park; one feels that modernist Benjamin Franklin would have approved.

Down the cobble walk, Franklin Court opens onto Chestnut Street, across from the reconstructed Pemberton home, now the Army and Navy Museum. In 1811 the home of Israel Pemberton was described as "laid out in the old fashioned style of uniformity, with walks and allees nodding to their brothers, and decorated with a number of evergreens carefully clipped into pyramidal and conical forms." Thus the trees, gardens and even weeds scattered through these landscapes recall past images and echo the voices of the founders of the nation.

Independence National Historical Park is administered by the National Park Service, Department of the Interior, and is open 365 days a year for visitors who make their pilgrimage to this national shrine.

Chapter 7

The Garden as Preserve

Inevitably we return to the garden as our most powerful and persistent metaphor for how we want to shape our place in nature

OVERLEAF: *Schuylkill Valley Nature Center*

THROUGH THE FIVE garden preserves profiled in this chapter, we see how far we have come in the 300-year struggle to find our place in nature. Like the other gardens of the Delaware Valley, they reveal the passion of one or a few people to preserve a piece of history or nature. As preserves, however, they quickly become community or collective enterprises, and in the Delaware Valley these take on several forms: landscape arboretum, wildflower garden, woodland, woodland overlaid with wildflowers and tidal water garden.

These five preserves offer a cross section, as few other places in this country could, of our changing attitudes toward nature and the varying approaches we have taken in dealing with these changes. In some cases, individuals have been moved to private acts of public generosity. In other cases, municipal, state and federal agencies, along with private conservancies, have been pressed into service to save our historic landscape.

In the Taylor Arboretum and Schuylkill Valley Nature Center for Environmental Education, individual initiatives find expression: Joshua Taylor in a garden preserve to honor the memory of a loved one, and two granddaughters of Henry Howard Houston in an environmental education center to preserve the memory of a rapidly vanishing landscape. The Brandywine Conservancy Garden, Bowman's Hill Wildflower Preserve and the John Heinz Wildlife Refuge at Tinicum also point to a few individuals who held the vision and had the imagination and energy to institutionalize these gardens.

Since 1986 the Natural Lands Trust has managed the Taylor Arboretum. The Trust is a non-profit organization based in Media, Pennsylvania, providing innovative approaches to landowners to develop strategies for acquisition, land use planning and management for preserving properties that have natural values. Founded in 1961, the Trust is the offspring of the Philadelphia Conservationists founded in 1953 as an organization to concentrate on land acquisition for preservation purposes. The saving of Tinicum Marsh in the early 1950s was their call to arms.

The operating assumption of the Philadelphia Conservationists was that once these lands had been acquired, they could then be turned over to government agencies to be managed. When it became clear that this would not happen, the Natural

Lands Trust was formed. The Trust is credited with the preservation of 40,000 acres since it was founded. The 32-acre Taylor Arboretum, 180-acre Gwynedd Wildlife Preserve and the 165-acre Walkinweir Preserve are among the 13,000 acres that the Trust holds title to and manages.

The Brandywine Conservancy River Museum grew up on the banks of another picturesque, historic river. The descent of the Brandywine on its way to the Delaware River made it a ready source of power in colonial times. The first mill was placed on the stream in the late 17th century and by the time of the War for Independence the Brandywine had aged into one of the most productive agricultural and manufacturing regions of this country. Its strategic position as a base for the British forces commanded by General William Howe on his way to occupy Philadelphia, was to forever stamp this land in our history books. The Battle of the Brandywine was fought on September 11, 1777. One thousand soldiers of Washington's Continental Army were killed or wounded in that battle, after which they re-engaged the British on October 4 in the Battle of Germantown. From that engagement the Continental Army retreated to spend a bitter winter at Valley Forge while General Howe was wined and dined in Philadelphia.

In the 1880s this picturesque landscape, marked with its hills, mills and history, attracted Howard Pyle (1853–1911). Author and illustrator of many popular children's books, he founded the Brandywine School of painters. N. C. Wyeth (1882–1945), one of his most successful students, passed his talent on to his son Andrew and grandson Jamie. Painters of the Brandywine School drew their inspiration from the land and in so doing propagated an image of this landscape.

By the mid 1960s it was clear that the painters' image was changing rapidly and that something had to be done to control unplanned growth of the region. The Brandywine Conservancy was founded in 1967, and in 1971 the Brandywine Museum opened its doors. George A. Weymouth, a du Pont on his mother's side and accomplished painter in his own right, has headed both Conservancy and Museum since their inception. In a 1985 article he declared, "We realized that the art was the crucial element in conserving the landscape."

Unlike the Natural Lands Trust, the Brandywine Conservancy does not manage

For the Natural Lands Trust that manages the Taylor Memorial Arboretum, land-use planning and development of preserves is a team approach

lands; it is in the business of assisting private landowners to better manage their properties to preserve natural values in perpetuity. Since it was founded, the Brandywine Conservancy has managed to place under conservation easement more than 25,000 acres and to list on its inventory of historic places more than 10,000 sites. The Brandywine Conservancy Garden in the vicinity of the Museum symbolizes the Conservancy's interest in the preservation of the landscape. The use of native flora is designed to resonate with the works of art inside the Museum, reflecting George Weymouth's principle of the relationship between art and nature.

Philadelphia's railroad magnate, Henry Howard Houston (1820–1895), acquired the Schuylkill Nature Center lands in 1886. His son, Samuel Frederic (1866–1952), inherited these lands and continued to view them as his father had, for their development potential. In 1926 he proposed a railroad link with this region and Bryn Mawr, and in 1947 made a pitch for having the United Nations build their headquarters here. (The U.N. chose a more favorable site on Manhattan Island, thanks to the generosity of the Rockefellers.)

It was left to Samuel Houston's daughters, however, to ultimately determine the fate of this property. Their interests lay in the area of conservation rather than development. Eleanor Houston Smith (1910–1987) and her sister, Margaret Houston Meigs (1891–1970), inherited both a family philanthropic tradition and a love of nature. The two sisters established a model of community planning by creating an urban environmental education center. The Schuylkill Valley Nature Center was founded in 1965 and began operations on July 1 of that year.

Another model of planning, this time on the state level, gave rise to the Bowman's Hill Wildflower Preserve. The idea was suggested by local botanists Edgar Wherry and John M. Fogg, who were well acquainted with the natural richness of the flora around Pidcock Creek, whose waters served as a source of power like the Brandywine. The dam and mill race are still visible elements in the landscape. While the natural endowment of the site provided the inspiration, the presence of Washington Crossing State Park established in 1917 provided the institutional framework within which such a preserve might develop. In 1934 Bowman's Hill Wildflower Preserve was created as a part of the park. As classroom, a source of propagating materials and quiet retreat, Bowman's Hill offers a glimpse of the gardens of the future: tended spaces designed to serve both for recreation and education, and as a resource for research while preserving the state's natural patrimony.

Preserving our natural patrimony is also the business of the John Heinz Wildlife Refuge at Tinicum. Tinicum Marsh is a system in flux in many different ways. Impoundment, landfill, dredging and practically every other imaginable insult has been heaped upon it as the city soaked up the surrounding area. In the 1950s Gulf Oil Co. had designs on the area as a settling basin for dredge spoil from the Schuylkill. In 1955 the Philadelphia Conservationists convinced Gulf Oil to donate to the City of Philadelphia 145 acres around the impoundment as the Tinicum Wildlife Preserve. It was a step in the right direction, but left the surrounding tidal marsh which contained much of the nesting habitat unprotected. In 1972 Congress passed Public Law 92-326 authorizing the Interior Department to acquire up to 1,200 acres to establish the

Tinicum Marsh Environmental Center under the U.S. Fish and Wildlife Service. In 1991 it was renamed the John Heinz Wildlife Refuge at Tinicum in honor of the Pennsylvania senator killed in a plane crash.

The unifying theme linking all five preserves is their commitment to education, to increasing the public's understanding of nature and our role as stewards of the land. They have all become classrooms and laboratories, challenging our ignorance of the diversity of living things and the fragility of the small remnants of our national heritage that survive from one generation to the next. They reflect in varying ways the growing sense of urgency that we are consuming and defiling our habitat. They also confront us with the eternal quest to find beauty in our lives, and from this vantage point we are able to see that in 300 years we have gone from fencing nature out to fencing nature in, to making the preservation of nature an act of gardening. The garden remains, in the words of art historian Sir Kenneth Clark, "one of humanity's most constant, widespread and consoling myths."

Only vestiges, less than 5 per cent of the original 5700 acres, remain of what was once Tinicum Marsh, a freshwater tidal system

These preserves confront us with our ignorance of the diversity of living things, the complexity of the interactions and the weakness of our predictive powers to forecast the consequences of our many and varied assaults upon our environment

Taylor Memorial Arboretum

Health, enjoyment and education of the public in perpetuity.

JOSHUA TAYLOR

*Bald Cypress (*Taxodium distichum*)*

THE TAYLOR MEMORIAL ARBORETUM is located in the western suburbs of Philadelphia, bounded by Chester Park on three sides and Ridley Creek to the south. It is the legacy of Joshua Charles Taylor (1873–1946), created in memory of his wife, Anne Rulon Gray. Although the landscape style of this well-protected 32-acre refuge is more closely related to that of collectors' gardens, it is treated as a preserve because of its management by the Natural Lands Trust.

Exploration of this arboreal preserve begins to the south of the Education Center, located at the entrance. The path leads down the hillside through the azalea and boxwood gardens below the fragrant Pine Hill (planted by Joshua Taylor) and into the West Wood. The unclipped boxes, collection of hybrid azaleas, variety of specimen plants and natural landscape contribute to its style as a landscape garden in the English tradition. It is a fitting tribute to Taylor, an Englishman who came to the United States in 1879 at the age of six and went on to success and fortune as a banker and lawyer. As a true Englishman, he made his garden his legacy.

West, South and East Woods border Ridley Creek and brace the Upland, Sedge and Floodplain Meadows. The Cross Trails, Rhododendron Walk and Azalea Trail are drawn through the landscape to reveal the many fine specimens to their best advantage: *Acer Davidii*, dawn redwood, *Cornus controversa*. Collections of crabapples, dogwoods, magnolias and maples edge the meadows to emphasize that this is indeed an arboretum preserve.

For nearly 200 years members of the Sharpless family operated their water-powered mills along Ridley Creek

The Arboretum is the last remnant of an 1,000-acre tract of land purchased in 1682 from William Penn by the Sharpless family. For nearly 200 years Sharpless descendants operated their water-powered mills along Ridley Creek. The dam site and mill race lined with azaleas and rhododendrons date to the mid-18th century. An old quarry has been converted into Anne's Grotto, named for Joshua Taylor's wife, a moss and lichen-covered rock wall framed with ferns and woodland flowers. Springs trace a course lined with trout lily and Solomon's seal to the pond ringed with Bald Cypress.

A "Preliminary Plan" dated March 1952 signed by Wendell H. Camp prefigures the present design. A botanist with the Academy of Natural Sciences, Dr. Camp was the first director when the Taylor Arboretum opened its gates in 1951. The design, building upon the natural and historic elements of this working mill site, tells a story of how technology is transformed into the gardenesque, reminiscent of the du Pont story as seen at Hagley Mills and the Crowninshield garden.

The Taylor Arboretum is managed by the Natural Lands Trust, which also manages approximately 13,000 acres including Hildacy Farm in Media (headquarters of the Trust), Gwynedd Wildlife Preserve (a 180-acre preserve in Upper Gwynedd Township) and Walkinweir Preserve, a 165-acre preserve in Pottstown, Pennsylvania, that was a rundown farm during the Depression and was nurtured back to garden preserve.

And from this vantage point we are able to see that in 300 years we have gone from fencing nature out to fencing nature in, to making the preservation of nature an act of gardening

"We realized that the art was the crucial element in preserving the landscape."   GEORGE A. WEYMOUTH

Brandywine Conservancy
River Museum

It's not the landscape itself that created the art,
it is the art that makes us see the landscape
a new way.

GEORGE A. WEYMOUTH, 1985

THE HEADQUARTERS of the Brandywine Conservancy is located in Chadds Ford, Pennsylvania. The stark, four-story, red brick pre-Civil War mill that dominates the view down Hoffman's Mill Road is now the Brandywine River Museum operated by the Brandywine Conservancy. Inside, the works of Howard Pyle, three generations of Wyeths, Frank Schoonover, Violet Oakley and others of what is known as the Brandywine School of painters, are exhibited in galleries renovated into a man-made state-of-the-art museum. Outside, the works of nature which inspired the famous Brandywine painters are on exhibit in galleries designed by nature.

The parking lot and area around the museum is a demonstration garden preserve established in 1974. Featuring more than 200 native and naturalized species of the Brandywine flora in island beds, this unique garden has a special resonance with the art of this area. Each bed features plants which have some special reason for being there, and the pond garden serves as a storm water detention basin. This is not the typical nature preserve but a special garden created to promote the objectives of the Conservancy: preserving an American heritage through land stewardship, environmental management and historic preservation.

Plantings around the museum have been selected with a view to providing color throughout the seasons. Spring is announced with bloodroot (*Sanguinaria canadensis*), Virginia bluebell (*Mertensia virginica*) and several species of Phlox (*P. divaricata*, *P. stolonifera* and *P. glaberrima*). Summer advances with sundrops (*Oenothera fruticosa*), butterfly weed (*Asclepias tuberosa*), coneflowers (*Rudbeckia*

Lilium superbum

287

triloba, *R. speciosa*, *R. laciniata*) and Cardinal flowers (*Lobelia cardinalis*). Fall is ushered in with the leaves of the tupelo (*Nyssa sylvatica*), shining sumac (*Rhus copallina*), downy serviceberry (*Amelanchier arborea*) and the goldenrods (*Solidago caesia*, *S. canadensis*). Winter color comes with the berries of American holly (*Ilex opaca*), inkberry (*Ilex glabra*) and the bark of sycamore (*Platanus occidentalis*) and river birch (*Betula nigra*).

Two small nursery areas are maintained near the Environmental Management Center and behind the Membership and Garden Offices. These buildings are also landscaped to demonstrate and encourage the wider use of native plants. More than 100 species are offered on the Brandywine seed list, one of the largest sources for wildflower seed in the region.

The path along the east side of the Brandywine Creek offers scenic views up this picturesque stream, a favorite for fishermen and canoeists. Continuing on this path a boardwalk zigs and zags across marshy riparian woodland through bog and on to a meadow edge. Across the meadow, perched on the hillside, is the home of John Chadd, built ca. 1726, the man who gave this place its name. From the Chadd house this pastoral landscape comes into splendid view. This is the site of the Brandywine battlefield where George Washington fought General Howe and then beat a strategic retreat in September 1777.

The Brandywine Conservancy Garden was planned, planted and is maintained by volunteers under the supervision of a Conservancy horticulturalist. In 1979 it was dedicated to two founding members of the Conservancy, Ford B. Draper and Henry A. Thouron.

The twists and turns of a society convulsed by change are on display here—outside turned in and inside turned out, nature into art and art turning nature into a preserve

Today the declaration from Philadelphia to the world must be one of our total interdependence

Schuylkill Valley Nature Center for Environmental Education

The environmental conscience of the city.

Jack-O-Lantern mushrooms

THIS COUNTRY'S first urban center for environmental education and still one of the nation's leaders in the field is located in the extreme northwestern section of the city of Philadelphia. This undulating green patch, stitching together the city's past with its future, varies in elevation from about 90 to 440 feet above sea level with three upland plateaus dissected by two ravines that empty their contents into the Schuylkill.

On the maps of the city of Philadelphia the Schuylkill Valley Nature Center appears as if it were a green postage stamp. It covers an area of seven city blocks; within its bounds 197 habitats have been identified. One of those 197 includes the woodland along the Ravine Trail where the pinxterbloom azalea (*Rhododendron perclymedoides*) sends out its pale pink blooms. Nearby the water gurgles over ancient stone.

The mixture of crooked, spindly hardwoods that line the entrance road are the great-great-great-grandchildren of a onetime great upland Piedmont forest. Along the entrance the low, crumbling dry stone wall, flecked with mica from the local Wissahickon schist, is now all but lost in the trees, a faint reminder of the limits of once-tended farmland.

With cinderblock construction in several modules over the years there is a no-frills, low-tech sense to the spaces and exhibits. Inside the Nature Center are classrooms, laboratories, libraries and one of the region's best-stocked natural history bookshops. Simple exhibits invite exploration of the fragments of nature that have been gathered, such as a slice of pond in a plexiglas sandwich that hangs at the window near an observation port for viewing bees. The daily pulse of atmospheric

Here life teems and whirrs with motion at all levels of observation from the microscopic to the cosmic

conditions is read by a weather station located near the headquarters building. A large "Eco Van" started full-time operation in 1988. It is equipped with experiments and exercises to assist schoolteachers in environmental education programs.

Outside is a 170 acre public classroom and teaching laboratory, the balance of the 500 acres that comprise SVNC in habitat preservation and community garden. The Upper Fields Trail takes off from the main buildings in a westerly direction toward the Schuylkill to connect with the Ravine Loop Trail, which gently arcs down slope between old and new growth forest. A small stream, paralleling Port Royal Avenue, courses over ancient rock and through forest as it makes its way to the river.

The area is naturally rich in wildlife, although the composition has changed dramatically over the last 300 years. Black bear, lynx, mountain lion and wild turkey have given way to deer and gray squirrels. Estimates place the deer population here at 1,300 and the carrying capacity of the Nature Center at about 40. Deer exclusion plots in the form of specially-constructed fences have been installed as part of a protective strategy.

The Schuylkill Valley Nature Center is a private not-for-profit organization, founded in 1965 with the donation of the land by Eleanor Houston Smith and Margaret Houston Meigs, sisters and heirs to the fortune of Pennsylvania Railroad entrepreneur Howard Houston. Many pioneering environmental education programs have started here, including graduate degree offerings through local colleges and institutions.

The message that rings out: we are connected to that space beyond this room and to all of the out-of-doors

An ancient rear guard presides over a scene that has long since vanished over the hill

Bowman's Hill Wildflower Preserve

The good gardener commonly borrows his methods, if not his goals, from nature herself.

MICHAEL POLLAN, *Second Nature*

BOWMAN'S HILL is a State preserve located in Bucks County on Pidcock Creek, a tributary of the Delaware River, approximately 15 miles north of Philadelphia. The entrance is off one of the most scenic river roads (Highway 32) in Pennsylvania, five miles north of historic Washington Crossing.

Within this 100-acre preserve 640 species of native plants are tended in 26 named wildflower gardens. Most of these gardens feature genera that have contributed much to the horticulture of the region: asters, bluebells, cornus, gentians, holly, laurel, marsh marigolds and a sprinkling of violets throughout. Other garden walks highlight habitat types: barrens, forest, meadow, pond and sphagnum bog. There are over 12 trails, including those that commemorate early naturalists Audubon and Parry. Two faculty members of the botany department of the University of Pennsylvania who were instrumental in establishing this wildflower preserve in the 1930s are also immortalized here: the Edgar Wherry Fern Trail and the Harshberger Trail.

The upland forests that once grew here have long since been cut, recut and cut again until there is nothing resembling the magnificent mixture of oaks and other hardwood trees that once dominated the region. A few remnants can still be seen in the hemlock stand at Bowman's Hill. One stately specimen was a sapling when Washington crossed the Delaware River and posted a lookout on Bowman's Hill. A few miles from Bowman's Hill a magnificent, gnarled old oak, dated 1492, stands alone in a field, adding one growth ring to its girth each year since Columbus discovered the New World.

"For the garden is a place with long experience of questions having to do with man in nature."   MICHAEL POLLAN

On October 12, 1944, in celebration of the 300th anniversary of the birth of William Penn, a nine-acre arboretum, Penn's Wood, was dedicated at the entrance to Bowman's Hill. Sixty-five species now grow in this memorial forest, which has become a popular place for students to gather leaves and fruits in the fulfillment of class assignments.

Birds are a major reason why visitors come to Bowman's Hill. The various species indicate the presence of certain types of habitat, such as woods, swamps and meadows. The application of minimally toxic pesticides at maximally effective times in the preserve ensures that the plants are protected and also that there is an abundance of insects as food for the resident bird population.

A growing concern over the sources of native plants led to the construction in 1984 of a propagation facility near the headquarters. It has been expanded in recent years to accommodate the increasing demand for wildflowers and to restock the exhibition gardens. It is unlike any other nursery, with approximately 200 species propagated from about 300 collections. Seeds are mostly collected on the preserve, although there are occasional rescue operations of plants under threat elsewhere. In addition to providing regeneration stock, the harvesting of seed also fuels an active seed exchange program with institutions throughout the world.

Twenty-six sponsors, mostly local garden clubs, have adopted each of the garden walks. Nature is not left to her own devices here. Wire cages envelop the yellow ladyslipper, azalea and trillium. A fence is being installed around the entire property to keep the deer

A Noah's Ark for our time is being constructed here against a flood tide about to swamp a rudderless society

out. Bowman's Hill is the prime example of gardeners taking responsibility for the preservation of nature.

Bowman's Hill Wildflower Preserve was founded in 1934 and is administered by the Washington Crossing Park Commission and the Pennsylvania Historical and Museum Commission in cooperation with Bowman's Hill Wildflower Preserve Assocation Inc., the volunteer arm of the civil service employees. Indoor classrooms, an exhibition gallery and gift shop are housed in the Headquarters Building.

The largest remaining fresh-water tidal marsh in Pennsylvania

John Heinz Wildlife Refuge at Tinicum

The highly disturbed condition of much of these lands presents an unusual opportunity as well as a challenge, to recreate the environments that formerly existed.

TINICUM MASTER PLAN, 1983

TINICUM NATIONAL ENVIRONMENTAL CENTER covers an area of 900 acres and includes the largest remaining fresh-water tidal marsh in Pennsylvania. Bounded on the north by Darby Creek, a tributary of the Delaware River, and south by I-95, it is a water garden that bathes the extreme southwest corner of the city of Philadelphia.

From the visitor center, mounted with weather-monitoring apparatus, the roadway extends in a westward direction along the dike of a large impoundment. At this point a glance up Darby Creek reveals the tidal influence: a head of water ranging over five feet at the mouth of the channel and spreading six miles up the stream bed, slightly north of the 84th Street bridge. The dike road arcs gently southward through lush growth of introduced and native trees: American ash (*Fraxinus americana*), boxelder (*Acer negundo*), paulownia (*Paulownia tomentosa*), black locust (*Robinia psuedo-acacia*), willow (*Salix sp.*), Norway maple (*Acer platanoides*), pie cherry (*Prunus cerasus*) and chokecherry (*Prunus virginiana*).

West of the impoundment (constructed between 1933 and 1935) the dike defines the southern bank of Darby Creek. The dissected pattern of the tidal marsh at low tide stretches out to the north in ribbons of green: banners of reed grass (*Phragmites communis*) and bluish-green lances of cattail (*Typha angustifolia*) hedge the borders and yellow-green arrow-head (*Sagittaria*) and deep green of spatterdock (*Nuphar advena* or *N. luteum*) extrude into the flats like small patches of chard or lettuce.

Across the tidal marsh the mound of the now-inactive Folcroft landfill presses down upon the channel, oozing and dripping we know not what into this waterway. Such encroachments into the wetlands of this country have resulted in the loss of productivity of some of our nation's most critically threatened ecosystems. West of the tidal marsh flat Tinicum Refuge narrows to an area undergoing the landscape equivalent of a facelift. Long Hook Creek, after years of conforming to human imperatives, is being returned to a reasonable facsimile of its original channel. Downstream from the restoration the Refuge narrows into tidal lagoons caught in a triangle of two highways, a cloverleaf and the Darby Creek Channel. The lagoons were dredged in 1969–1970 to provide fill for I-95, the watery graves of Tinicum Island which once covered approximately one square mile of this area. On a spring morning the air is filled with the sounds of blackbirds, warblers, Canada geese and other birds. This choral ensemble numbers 288 kinds of vocalists, 50 of whom nest here.

Since 1972 the Tinicum Wildlife Refuge has been under the management of the U.S. Fish and Wildlife Service. It is one of 400 Wildlife Refuges that cover more than 90 million acres across this country. In 1991 it was renamed the John Heinz Wildlife Refuge at Tinicum in memory of the late Pennsylvania Senator.

In a litigious society, where preserves such as Tinicum are fenced by laws such as the Endangered Species Act of 1973, not knowing the names of the birds, trees and flowers can lead to their extinction

Other Preserves and Gardens of Interest in the Delaware Valley

NOTE: *Besides the gardens listed here, the Pennsylvania Horticultural Society, Hospitality Philadelphia Style and the Scott Foundation offer garden tours to members on a regular basis.*

NATURE PRESERVES

Ashland Nature Center
Headquarters
Delaware Nature Education Society
Brackenville & Barley Mill Roads
Hockessin, Delaware 19707

(302) 239–2334

600 acres of deciduous forests, rolling meadows, ponds, trails.

Briar Bush Nature Center
1212 Edge Hill Road
Abington, Pennsylvania 19001

(215) 887–6603

Native wildflower gardens, woodlands, bird-watching, hands-on exhibits.

Churchville Nature Center
501 Churchville Lane
Churchville, Pennsylvania 18966

(215) 357–4005

Meadow, marsh, woodland and fresh-water lake.

Five Mile Woods
Lower Makefield Township
Bucks County, Pennsylvania

(215) 493–3646

285 acres of wildflowers, trails, streams, woodland, mature forest.

Four Mills Nature Reserve
12 Morris Road
Ambler, Pennsylvania 19002

(215) 646–8866

Home of the Wissahickon Valley Watershed Association, founded to protect the Wissahickon Creek—nature walks and educational programs.

Mill Grove—The Audubon Wildlife Sanctuary
  Pawling Road
  Audubon, Pennsylvania 19407

  (215) 666–5593

  The first home of artist and naturalist John James Audubon, 130 acres of nature trails and woodland, with exhibits of Audubon's art.

Nature Center of Charlestown
  Rte. 29 and Hollow Road
  Phoenixville, Pennsylvania 19460

  (215) 935–9777

  Trails, hands-on nature exhibits, animals, workshops.

Peace Valley Nature Center
  130 Chapman Road
  Doylestown, Pennsylvania 18901

  (215) 345–7860

  Nine miles of trails, fields, woods, bird-watching.

Riverbend Environmental Educational Center
  Springmill Road
  Gladwyne, Pennsylvania 19035

  (215) 527–5234

  Twenty-six acres of woodland and fields, trails for hiking, riding, nature studies and cross-country skiing.

Valley Forge National Historical Park
  Valley Forge, Pennsylvania 19481

  (215) 783–7700

  The 1777–1778 winter encampment of George Washington's Continental Army, the park has living history exhibits and over 600 species of plants.

GARDENS

Belfield Farm
  20th and Belfield Avenue
  Germantown, Pennsylvania 19144

  Home of artist and naturalist Charles Wilson Peale, who designed the gardens from 1810 to 1826.

College of Physicians of Philadelphia
  19 South 22nd Street
  Philadelphia, Pennsylvania 19103

  (215) 563–3737

  Conceived by Dr. Benjamin Rush, this medicinal herb garden is planted in four parterres with shrubs and a plane tree from Greece.

Marshall's Botanic Garden
  Marshallton Village, Pennsylvania 19380

  (215) 692–4800

  Owned by the Chester County Historical Society, this is one of the earliest American gardens, founded in 1773 by Humphry Marshall, botanist and cousin of John Bartram.

Rockwood Museum
  610 Shipley Road
  Wilmington, Delaware 19809

  (302) 571–7776

  Nineteenth century country estate with 70 acres of grounds and landscaped gardens.

The Grange
  Myrtle Avenue at Warwick Road
  Havertown, Pennsylvania 09083

  (215) 446–4958

  A colonial estate dating from 1682 with hardwood forest, woodlands, rare trees, flowering shrubs and an acre of formal gardens.

US 202

7

N

I-95

Morrisville

I-276 PA Turnpike

28

4
town

US1 Roosevelt Blvd

Delaware River

2

nden

Legend

1 American College Arboretum

2 Andalusia

3 Appleford/Parsons-Banks

4 The Arboretum of the Barnes Foundation

5 Awbury Arboretum

6 Bartram's Garden

7 Bowman's Hill Wildflower Preserve

8 Brandywine Conservancy River Museum

9 Bryn Mawr College

10 Chanticleer

11 The Colonial Pennsylvania Plantation

12 Delaware Valley College

13 Doe Run Farm

14 Ebenezer Maxwell Mansion

15 Fairmount Park

16 Hagley Museum and Library

17 Haverford College Arboretum

18 The Henry Foundation for Botanical Research

19 The Highlands

20 Independence National Historical Park

21 Jenkins Arboretum

22 John Heinz Wildlife Refuge at Tinicum

23 Longwood Gardens

24 Meadowbrook Farm

25 Morris Arboretum

26 Mount Cuba

27 Nemours

28 Pennsbury Manor

29 Pennsylvania Horticultural Society

30 Pennsylvania Hospital Physic Garden

31 Pennypacker Mills

32 Peter Wentz Farmstead

33 Schuylkill Valley Nature Center

34 Scott Arboretum of Swarthmore College

35 Stenton

36 Swiss Pines

37 Taylor Memorial Arboretum

38 Temple University Ambler Campus

39 Tyler Arboretum

40 Wallingford Rose Garden

41 Winterthur

42 Wyck

43 Zoological Society of Philadelphia

Visitor's Guide to Gardens of Philadelphia & the Delaware Valley

Please note that the information provided below may have changed. Check with the gardens for up-to-date listings.

American College Arboretum

270 S. Bryn Mawr Avenue
Bryn Mawr, PA 19010

(610) 526-1100

Hours: Open dawn to dusk. Closed week between Christmas and New Year

Admission fees: None

Guided and group tours: Primarily self-guided; brochure available from Gregg Conference Center. Call for reservations

Facilities: Free parking, jogging course, restaurant at Gregg Conference Center (call for reservations), picnicking by pond, handicap access

Size of garden: 35 acres

Recommended time for visit: 1 hr.

Special events:
Art exhibitions in Gregg Conference Center Galleries, Monday–Friday 8–6

Seasonal highlights:
Spring: Azaleas, rhododendron, bulbs, dogwood
Summer: Deciduous trees, lawns, ponds and stream
Fall: Foliage color
Winter: Evergreens

Curator's choice: Collection of specimen trees; major buildings by Aldo Giurgola

Andalusia

Box 158
1237 State Road
Andalusia, PA 19020

(215) 639-2077

Hours: Open by appointment only. Closed all holidays

Admission fees:
Adults: $9 per person, minimum $48

Guided and group tours: Call for reservations

Facilities: Free parking

Size of garden: 30 acres

Special events: Approximately 3 events a year

Seasonal highlights:
Spring: Shrubs, borders
Summer: Roses, borders
Fall: Borders
Winter: Arboretum

Curator's choice: Walled garden

Appleford / Parsons-Banks Arboretum

770 Mt. Moro Road
Villanova, PA 19085

(215) 527-4280

Hours: Open daily until sunset, year-round

Admission fees: None

Guided and group tours: Call for reservations (available several times a year)

Facilities: Free parking, handicap access

Size of garden: 22 acres

Recommended time for visit: 1 hr.

Special events:
May: Garden and Tea Party; plant sale
December: Christmas Party

Seasonal highlights:
Spring: Bulbs, deciduous trees, ornamental trees, dogwoods, wisteria, wildflowers
Summer: Rock garden plants, perennials, roses, annuals, planted containers, standard hibiscus
Fall: Perennials, annuals, chrysanthemums, fall foliage

Curator's choice: Bird sanctuary

Awbury Arboretum

Francis Cope House
Philadelphia, PA 19138-1505
(Enter from Chew Avenue,
southeast of Washington Lane)

(215) 849-2855

Hours: Dawn to dusk, year-round

Admission fees: None

Guided and group tours: Call for
reservations

Facilities: Free parking, no handicap access to restrooms

Size of garden: 55 acres

Recommended time for visit: 2 hrs.

Special events:
May: Spring fair and plant sale
December: Christmas greens work-
shop and sale
Special lectures, workshops, educa-
tional trips throughout the year

Seasonal highlights:
Spring: Flowering bulbs, dogwood,
fruit trees, trout lilies, aconites,
snowdrops, wildflowers, warbler
migration
Summer: Bottlebrush-buckeye, lin-
den, sophors japonica, blackberries,
wineberries, cherries, red wing
blackbirds, hawks, owls
Fall: Franklinea in bloom, persim-
mons, sugar maples, tupelo, sour-
wood and other highly colored
trees and shrubs
Winter: Witchhazel, tours of bark,
buds and twigs

Curator's choice: Vistas and landscaping; large pond and wetland
eco-system; champion specimen
trees

Education: (1) Environmental Education Program, a year-round program serving children; *(2)* Summer
Nature Program: teaches children
through games, activities and gardening, as enrichment program for
nearby summer camp serving children from disadvantaged neighborhoods; *(3)* Outreach and loan box
programs. Call the education office
at (215) 849-5561

Arboretum of the Barnes Foundation

300 N. Latch's Lane
Merion, PA 19066

(215) 667-0290

Hours: Closed until fall 1995; hours
to be determined

Admission fees: N/A

Guided and group tours: Call for
reservations

Facilities: No parking, no handicap
access

Size of garden: 12 acres

Recommended time for visit:
60–90 min.

No pets / No bicycles

Seasonal highlights:
Spring: Magnolia, malus, lilacs
Summer: Roses, rock garden,
woodland ferns
Winter: Stewartia, dwarf conifers

Education: Three-year program in
horticulture, botany and landscape
design; lectures; workshops; sym-
posia. Write to the Barnes Foundation, 300 N. Latch's Lane, Merion,
PA 19066, or call (215) 664-8880

Bartram's Garden

54th Street and Lindbergh Blvd.
Philadelphia, PA 19143

(215) 729-5281

Hours: Grounds open dawn to
dusk free to the public

Admission fees:
House tours, adults: $3

Guided and group tours: Walk-in
tours: May–October, Wednesday–
Sunday 12–4; November–March,
Wednesday–Friday, 12–4. Tours
start at 10 minutes past the hour.
Group tours seven days/week with
advance reservation

Facilities: Bartram House and outbuildings, museum shop, picnicking pavilion, public restrooms, free
parking, limited handicap access

Size of garden:
8-acre colonial botanical garden
17-acre wildflower meadow
20-acre public recreation area

Recommended time for visit: 1–1½ hrs.

Special events:
May: Native plant sale
June: Schuylkill River Festival
December: Holiday greens sale

Seasonal highlights:
Spring: Bulbs and native flowering
trees and shrubs
Summer: Wildflower meadow,
period kitchen and flower gardens
Fall: Franklin trees in bloom,
autumn foliage
Winter: Birdwatching

Curator's choice: 200-plus year-old
ginkgo (*Ginkgo biloba*) and yellowwood (*Cladrastis kentuckea*); Franklin trees (*Franklinia alatamaha*)

Education: Year-round programs
for children combining history,
science and nature; annual Bartram
Trail tour, historical newsletter and
lectures for adults

Bowman's Hill Wildflower Preserve

Washington Crossing Historic Park
P.O. Box 103
Washington Crossing, PA 18977

(215) 862-2924

Hours: Open Monday–Saturday
9–5, Sunday 12–5. Closed New
Year's Day, Thanksgiving and
Christmas Day

Admission fees: None

Guided and group tours: Daily at 2,
March 1–October 31, or by reservation only

Facilities: Free parking, gift shop,
picnicking, handicap access, small
library

Size of garden: 80 acres

Recommended time for visit:
1 hour minimum

No pets / No bicycles on trails

Special events:
May: Wildflower weekend, spring
plant sale
November: Craft sale
December: Indoor holiday display

Seasonal highlights:
Spring: Woodland wildflowers
(April and May are peak bloom
times for traditional wildflowers)
Summer: Field and roadside
wildflowers (July is the best time to
see the fern collection)
Fall: Asters and goldenrods (October is the height of the foliage
color; Penn's Woods tree trail is
especially beautiful)
Winter: Evergreen trees, shrub and
ground covers; wild birds on trails
or at bird-feeding area

Curator's choice: Headquarters gardens highlight plants representative
of what is in bloom along the trails

Education: 2pm-daily public tour
during blooming season; wildflower identification classes
(March–October); Sunday lectures
during January and February

Brandywine Museum and Conservancy

Rt. One,
Chadds Ford, PA 19317

(610) 388-2700

Hours: 9:30–4:30, every day of the week. Closed Christmas Day

Admission fees:
Adults: $5 ($4 groups)
Children up to age 6 free
Senior Citizens: $2.50
Students: $2.50

Guided and group tours: Available Monday–Friday, 9:30–3:30. Call for reservation

Facilities: Free parking, gift shop, museum, restaurant (daily, 11 to 3), handicap access

Size of garden: 3 acres plus river trail

Recommended time for visit: 1 hr.

No pets
Bicycles on paths or in lot only

Special events:
May: Wildflower, native plant and seed sale; American antiques show
June: Brandywine bonsai show
September: Pennsylvania Craft Guild fall show
September–November: Fall harvest market
November–December: Christmas shops; a Brandywine Christmas

Seasonal highlights:
Spring: Bloodroot, bluebells, foamflower, spring-beauty, wood poppy, blue phlox, smooth phlox, sundrops, dogwoods, shadbush
Summer: 5 species of black-eyed Susans, crimson-eyed rose mallow, Turk's cap, Canada lily, cardinal flower, blue lobelia, dense blazing star, butterfly weed, trumpet vine
Fall: Pink turtleheads, Joe-Pye weed, tick-seed sunflower, New England aster, blackgum
Winter: American holly, inkberry, bayberry, sycamore, yellow fruited American holly

Curator's choice: The garden on the Museum's river side. Here the lines of the architecture, walkway and garden beds harmonize with those of the Brandywine River. Authentic millstones, which relate to the earliest function of the building, now serve as seats for relaxed, restful viewing of the river, the sculpture and the garden

Bryn Mawr College

Office of Events
Campus Center
Bryn Mawr, PA 19010-2899

(610) 526-7330

Hours: Open 9–5 daily. Closed Thanksgiving and Christmas

Admission fees: None

Guided and group tours: Call for reservations, (610) 526-7935

Facilities: Parking with visitor's permit, Campus Center book & gift shop, handicap access, Canaday Library, home of one of the finest collections of botanical illustrations, specializing in roses

Size of garden: 120 acres

Recommended time for visit: 1–2 hrs.

No pets / No bicycles

Special events:
May: traditional May Day Celebration including five maypole dances, a hoop roll, jesters, medieval plays. Throughout the year there are other events such as theatre, dance, music and lectures

Seasonal highlights:
Spring: April and early May display of cherries
Summer: Pastoral landscape with mature specimen trees
Fall: Changing leaf colors
Winter: Architecture becomes prominent

Curator's choice: First example of collegiate Gothic architecture, surrounded by mature trees. Not to be missed are *Quercus rubra*, *Prunus avium* and *Platanus occidentalis*

Chanticleer

786 Church Road
Wayne, PA 19087

(610) 687-4163

Hours: April–October, Wednesday–Saturday, 10 to 3:30

Admission fees:
Adults: $5
Children 12–16 years: $3

Guided and group tours: By appointment Wednesday and Thursday. Call for reservations

Facilities: Free parking

Size of garden: 32 acres

Recommended time for visit: 1½–2 hrs.

No pets / No bicycles

Special events: 2 or 3 fundraising events held throughout the summer

Seasonal highlights:
Spring: Flowering exotics and natives, bulbs
Summer: Herbaceous perennials
Fall: Perennials, tree and shrub color

Curator's choice: Fine herbaceous and rose gardens, unusual plant collections, estate production areas including vegetable garden

Education: Currently offering programs for other institutions such as Pennsylvania Horticultural Society

Colonial Pennsylvania Plantation

Ridley Creek State Park
Media, PA 19063

(215) 566-1725

Hours: Mid-April to mid-November 10–5, Saturday–Sunday. Groups only by appointment. Closed mid-November to mid-April

Admission fees:
Adults: $3
Children 4–12 years: $2
Senior Citizens: $2
Group discounts: weekends only

Guided and group tours: Tuesday–Saturday, 9:30–4:00. Call for reservations

Facilities: Free parking, gift shop, picnicking, handicap access limited, library

Size of garden: ½ acre

Recommended time for visit: 1 hr.

No pets / No bicycles

Special events:
May: Colonial Fair – traditional craft show
June: Kids Day
July: Civil War reenactment
September: Court Day
October: Harvest Feast; Fall Fun Day

Seasonal highlights:
Spring: Seeds of early vegetables in prepared beds; harvesting of root vegetables
Summer: Planting of late spring vegetables and herb seeds and plants
Fall: Harvesting of vegetables; storing and preserving for winter – cabbage, potatoes, onions; drying of beans

Curator's choice: Flax, tobacco, bedstraw, equisetum, scarlet runner beans

Delware Valley College, Henry Schmieder Arboretum

700 E. Butler Avenue
Doylestown, PA 18901

(215) 345-1500, ext. 2244

Hours: Open year-round

Admission fees: None

Guided and group tours: Call for reservations

Facilities: Free parking, student store, library specializing in ornamental horticulture

Size of garden: 45 acres

Recommended time for visit: 2 hrs.

No pets

Special events:
Spring and fall lecture series
A-Day (last weekend in April): 2 days of mostly agricultural events including sheep-shearing, cattle judging, floral arrangements, etc.

Seasonal highlights:
Spring: Bulbs
Summer: Annuals
Fall: Mums and ornamental kale

Curator's choice: 350-year old sycamore; new vine garden

Education: Day and evening college classes for credit

Doe Run Farm

R.D. 5, Thouron Road
Unionville, PA 19375

(610) 384-5542

Hours: Open by appointment only

Admission fees: None (no children)

Guided and group tours: Limited to 30 persons by appointment only. Call for reservations

Facilities: Limited parking

Size of garden: (not public) 15 acres

Recommended time for visit: 1¼ hrs.

Seasonal highlights: Summer

Curator's choice: British-style garden architecture

Ebenezer Maxwell Mansion

200 W. Tulpehocken Street
Philadelphia, PA 19144

(215) 438-1861

Hours: Open Thursdays–Sundays 1–4, April–mid-December. Closed mid-December–March

Admission fees:
Adults: $4
Children: $2
Students: $2
Discounts for groups: $3 per person for groups of 10 or more

Guided and group tours: Thursday–Sunday 1–4, by appointment. Call for reservations

Facilities: On-street parking, picnicking on grounds with prior consent

Size of garden: ¼ acre

Recommended time for visit: 1 hr. for house and garden

No pets / No bicycles

Special events:
Spring: Annual fund-raising dinner
Summer: Victorian Ice Cream Social
Fall: Philadelphia Old House Fair

Seasonal highlights:
Spring, summer and fall are best times to visit garden

Curator's choice: Ribbon garden; cast-iron deer by pond and rockwork; hemlock arch

Education: Restoration workshops throughout the year for 19th-century faux finishing techniques of woodgraining, marbleizing and trompe l'oeil

Fairmount Park

N. Horticultural Drive &
Montgomery Drive
Philadelphia, PA 19131

(215) 685-0096 *fax:* (215) 879-4062

Hours: Open 9–3 daily. Closed
all official City holidays

Admission fees:
Horticulture Center: $1 per person
Japanese House: $2.75 per person

Guided and group tours: Japanese
House only, April–October.
Call for reservations (215) 685-0104
or (215) 878-5097

Facilities: Free parking, gift shop,
picnicking by permit only, handicap access

Size of garden: 22½ acres

Recommended time for visit: 4 hrs.

No pets / bicycles only on main
roads

Special events:
April: Arbor Week activities
May: Historic houses in flower
tour
September: Fall Harvest Show by
Pennsylvania Horticultural Society
November/December: Park house
Christmas tours

Seasonal highlights:
Spring: Bulbs, magnolias, crabapples, cherries, azaleas, Easter lilies
Summer: Franklinia collection,
evodia, summer annuals; medicinal
and culinary herb exhibit; vegetable
garden of tomatoes, raspberries,
blueberries, asparagus; tuberous
garden of flags, gladiolus, canns,
cladiums
Fall: Chrysanthemums, fall colors
Winter: Winter berries, evergreens;
icy creeks

Curator's choice: Kalopanax pictus –
Aralia tree – rare specimen; *Betula
maxmowicziana* – grove of large
white barked trees; magnolia
species; *Tsuga canadensis pendula*
grove; Japanese House azalea
collection

Hagley Museum and Library

Route 141, P.O. Box 3630
Wilmington, DE 19807

(302) 658-2400

Hours: Open daily March 15–
December 30 and January 1, 9:30–
4:30. January 2–March 14 the mu-
seum is open weekends, 9:30–4:30.
Winter weekdays there is one
guided tour at 1:30 pm. Closed
Thanksgiving, Christmas and New
Year's Eve

Admission fees:
Adults: $9.75
Children 6–14: $3.50 (under 6, free)
Senior Citizens and Students: $7.50
Groups: Adult group tours (vari-
ous options) $6.50 – $12.50 (15 or
more people); student groups
$2.50–$5.50 (15 or more people)

Guided and group tours: Available
9:30–4:30 on all open days. Call for
reservations

Facilities: Free parking, gift shop,
coffee shop open 11–4 (closed
January–mid-March), picnicking,
partially accessible to people with
disabilities, library specializing in
technology, industrial and economic history

Size of property: 240 acres

Recommended time for visit: 3 4 hrs.

No pets / No bicycles

Special events:
April: Storybook Garden Party
June: Fireworks at Hagley
(members only)
August: Summer Blast
October: Craft Fair
November: Festival of Museum
Shopping
December: Christmas at Hagley

Seasonal highlights:
Spring: Masses of flowering trees,
shrubs, bulbs and wildflowers
Summer: Heirloom vegetables, an-
nuals and perennials in the E. I. du
Pont Restored Garden & Workers'
Garden
Fall: Fall color from the variety of
native and exotic trees; chrysanthe-
mums in the E. I. du Pont Restored
Garden
Winter: Flower arrangements in-
side the residence and potted plants

Curator's choice: Espaliered varieties
of historic fruit trees; dramatic garden landscape of the Brandywine
valley; specimen trees such as
Osage Orange (*Maclura pomifera*)

Education: Hagley's Education
Department offers a variety of focus tours and programs which explore the stories of industrializa-
tion, waterpower and community
life. Contact Coordinator of Education, (302) 658-2400, ext. 285

Haverford College Arboretum

370 Lancaster Avenue
Haverford, PA 19041-1392

(215) 896-1101

Hours: Dawn to dusk year-round

Admission fees: None

Guided and group tours: Seasonal
tours upon request. Call for
reservations

Facilities: Free parking, college book
store, restaurant, 7:30–10, 11–1:30,
5–7, picnicking upon request, handicap access limited, library

Size of garden: 216 acres

Recommended time for visit: 1–1½hrs.

Pets discouraged

Special events:
September: New members' recep-
tion and campus tour
October: Two-day garden trip, tree
identification course
November: Members' evening
January: Winter tour
February: Illustrated lecture and
reception
March: Garden symposium on
landscape design
April: Tree identification course,
Arbor Day celebration, plant divi-
dend day
May: Local garden visit

Seasonal highlights:
Spring: Ornamental fruit trees,
azaleas, rhododendrons, flowering
native trees, Fletcher-Silver walk
Summer: Smith-Magill Gardens,
sculpture gardens, duck pond
Fall: Maple and oak collections, fall
fruiting shrubs
Winter: Pinetum, structural outlines of mature trees, Japanese Zen
garden, arborvitae maze

Curator's choice: Three state champion trees; Reptonian landscape
with many mature trees; Carvill
arch; Penn Treaty Elm descendant;
Recumbent Maclura pomifera

Education: Tree identification
course "Knowing Your Trees"

Henry Foundation for Botanical Research

801 Stony Lane
Gladwyne, PA 19035

(610) 525-2037

Hours: Monday–Friday 10–4; weekends by appointment

Admission fees: None

Guided and group tours: Call for reservations

Facilities: Limited parking, no handicap access to garden, botanical library (in house use)

Size of garden: 50 acres

No pets or bicycles

Special events: Art exhibits, photography workshops, seasonal tours, rare plant sales in May and October

Seasonal highlights:
Spring: Native plants include species of magnolias, rhododendrons, wildflowers, halesia, aesculus, styrax, chionanthus, wisteria and herbaceous material
Summer: Herbaceous material and vines
Fall: Herbaceous material in rock garden—*Eriogonum alleni*, asters, vacciniums
Winter: species of Ilex, Symplocos and Amaryllidaceae

Native magnolia collection is registered with the AABGA North American Plant Collection Consortium

Magnolia ashei—national champion

Education: Series of classes and lectures on native plants, botanical illustration, orchids, pruning, etc.

The Highlands

7001 Sheaff Lane
Fort Washington, PA 19034

(215) 641-2687

Hours: Monday–Friday 9–4; weekends by appointment. Tours of the Mansion and Gardens, appointments preferred. Gardens open daily year-round

Admission fees: Donation recommended; $3 per person for tours

Guided and group tours: Monday–Friday 9–4 or by appointment on weekends. Call for reservations

Facilities: Free parking, picnicking, handicap access limited in mansion, library with limited materials

Size of garden: 44 acres, enclosed walled garden 4 acres

Recommended time for visit: 45 min. to 1 hr.

Bus parking area / Pets outside only
Bicycles outside only

Special events:
April: Quilt show (alternate years)
May: Garden Party and Herb Sale
June: "Glyndebourne" musical picnic and concert
July: Rug hooking school
September: Jazz concert
October: Craft Show
November: Hunt Breakfast
January: Concert series
February: Concert series
March: Rug hooking weekend

Seasonal highlights:
Spring: Bulbs and blossoming trees
Summer: Herb garden and flower beds in bloom
Fall: Spectacular leaf display
Winter: Architectural features of garden

Curator's choice: Springhouse, Gardener's Cottage, 3-story Barn

Education: Workshops offered in spring/fall

Independence National Historical Park

313 Walnut Street
Philadelphia, PA 19106

(215) 597-8974

Hours: Grounds open year-round, including holidays. Buildings open 9–5 daily with extended summer hours. Gardens open until dusk

Admission fees: None

Guided and group tours: Self-guided tours only

Facilities: Paid parking at adjacent garages, gift shop, restaurant, handicap access, library

Size of garden: 40 historic buildings and 7 gardens within a park setting of approximately 45 acres

Recommended time for visit: 1–2 days for the whole park. One day for the gardens only

Pets must be leashed / Bicycles must be walked

Seasonal highlights:
Spring: Magnolia garden and azaleas
Summer: Rose garden; old rose varieties bloom in early summer; 18th-century vegetable garden
Fall: Chrysanthemums at the Liberty Bell Pavilion
Winter: American holly trees in the Bishop White garden and throughout the park

Curator's choice: Independence Hall: site of the adoption of the Declaration of Independence and drafting of U.S. Constitution; Liberty Bell: symbol of American freedom; Franklin Court: site of Benjamin Franklin's house, archeology exhibit, post office, underground museum, printing office

Jenkins Arboretum

631 Berwyn Baptist Road
Devon, PA 19333

(610) 647-8870

Hours: Daily sunrise to sunset year-round

Admission fees: None

Guided and group tours: Call for reservations

Facilities: Free parking, picnicking limited to picnic area, handicap access limited to level areas

Size of garden: 46 acres, of which 15 acres are open to public

Recommended time for visit: 1½ hrs.

No pets / No bicycles or play equipment

Special events:
May: Spring plant sale

Seasonal highlights:
Spring: Early ephemeral woodland wildflowers; rhododendrons and azaleas in naturalized plantings
Summer: Woodland ecology and pond; over 400 varietes of daylilies during July
Fall: Species diversity of color in large trees, understory plants such as dogwoods and viburnums, deciduous azaleas, ferns, evergreens such as hollies and rhododendrons
Winter: Evergreens, exfoliating bark on trees

Curator's choice: In spring, especially May, the view from the grassy areas across the pond up the hill into the woodlands; hundreds of species of wildflowers, with colorful plantings of thousands of azaleas and rhododendrons

John Heinz Wildlife Refuge at Tinicum

86th and Lindbergh Boulevard
Philadelphia, PA 19153

(215) 365-3118

Hours: Gate open 8am–sunset

Admission fees: None

Guided and group tours: Weekends as scheduled. Groups must register in advance

Facilities: Free parking, handicap access, library for teachers only.

Size of garden: 1,200 acres

Seasonal highlights:
Spring: A wide variety of warblers, waterfowl, sandpipers and wading birds flying north during migration
Summer: Peak populations of herons, egrets and sandpipers; swamp rose mallow, crimson-eyed mallow in abundance
Fall: Sandpipers, warblers, waterfowl migrating south; muskrats, fall flowers
Winter: Hawks, sparrows and waterfowl, winter shapes of plants

Curator's choice: The largest remaining and most easily observed freshwater tidal marsh left in Pennsylvania. Habitat for wide variety of wetland plants

Education: Environmental Education workshops for teachers given in spring, summer and fall

Longwood Gardens

Route 1 (P.O. Box 501)
Kennett Square, PA 19348-0501

(610) 388-1000
(800) 737-5500 (for recorded information from CT, NY, NJ, PA, DE, MD, DC, VA)

Hours: Open year-round.
Outdoors: 9–6
(9–5 November–March)
The Conservatories: 10–6 (10–5 November–March)
Longwood is also open many evenings throughout the year

Admission fees:
Adults: $10 ($6 on Tuesdays)
Youths (ages 16–20): $6
Children (ages 6–15): $2
Under age 6: Free
Students (group with teacher): $2
Discounts for groups (30 minimum): $8 ($6 on Tuesdays)

Guided and group tours: Call for reservations

Facilities: Free parking, shop, restaurant, picnicking, handicap access, library

Size of garden: 1,050 acres

Recommended time for visit: Minimum of 2–3 hrs.

No pets / No bicycles

Special events:
January–April: Welcome Spring (indoors)
April–May: Acres of Spring (outdoors)
June–September: Festival of Fountains, plays, fireworks
September–October: Autumn's colors
November: Chrysanthemum Festival
December: Christmas display

Also 400 special concerts throughout the year

Seasonal highlights:
Spring: Welcome Spring (indoors) with a succession of 45,000 bulbs, acacias, orchids, palms, emerald green indoor lawns; (outdoors) a profusion of flowering bulbs, shrubs, trees and perennials in late spring
Summer: Annuals, perennials, vegetables, waterlilies, fountains, fireworks
Fall: Annuals, perennials, waterlilies, fall bulbs, glorious foliage, chrysanthemums
Winter: (indoors) poinsettias, bulbs, orchids, roses, tropicals, ferns, decorated Christmas trees; (outdoors) Christmas lighting display, witchhazels

Curator's choice: Conservatory (year-round); main fountain garden (spring–fall); open-air theatre fountains (spring–Christmas); Italian water garden; flower garden walk (spring–fall); Idea garden (spring–fall); waterlilies (summer–fall); Peirce's Park (year-round)

Education: Continuing Education; Professional Gardener Training Program; internships for college students; International Gardener Training Program

New additions indoors: Silver garden; Cascade garden (the only garden by Roberto Burle Marx in the U.S.) Mediterranean garden

Meadowbrook Farm

1633 Washington Lane
P.O. Box 3007
Meadowbrook, PA 19046

(215) 887-5900

Hours: Open only to garden and horticulture organizations in goups numbering 15 to 35 by appointment

Admission fees: None

Facilities: Free parking, gift shop

Size of garden: 5 acres

Recommended time for visit: 2 hrs.

No pets / No bicycles

Seasonal highlights:
Spring: Flowering shrubbery, bulbs, early annuals, perennial borders
Summer: Large assortment of tub and pot plants in flowers, hanging baskets
Fall: Late-flowering shrubbery, chrysanthemums
Winter: The perfect time to see and feel the "bones" of this highly-designed landscape

Curator's choice: The success of the garden design lies in its vistas, featuring focal points at the terminals of the main and cross axes

Education: Informal talks on garden design, perennials, pot plant culture, Christmas decorations, topiaries and pruning available to the visiting groups

Morris Arboretum of the University of Pennsylvania

100 Northwestern Avenue
Philadelphia, PA 19118

(215) 247-5777

Hours: Weekends, April–October:
10–5; weekends, November–
March: 10–4; weekdays, all year:
10–4. Open most holidays, but
closed Christmas Eve and New
Year's Day

Admission fees:
Adults: $3
Students: $1.50
Senior citizens: $1.50
Pre-schoolers and members: free

Guided and group tours: 2 pm weekends. Group tours by appointment
only. Call for reservations

Facilities: Free parking, snack/pic-
nic area, handicap access

Size of garden: 166 acres

Recommended time for visit: 1–2 hrs.

No bicycles / No pets

Special events:
May: Plant sale
June: Moonlight and Roses Gala
September: Musical concerts
October: Fall Festival
December: Holiday Party

Seasonal highlights:
Spring: Rhododendrons, azaleas,
magnolias, crabapples
Summer: Roses, cottage garden
Fall: Autumn foliage

Curator's choice: Over 8,000 labeled
woody plants; 20 state champion
big trees; sculpture garden, Victorian Fernery

Education: Programs include internships, school tours, courses in
arboriculture, landscape, horticulture and forestry; community outreach; workshops and conferences

Mount Cuba Center

(Please phone for directions)

(302) 239-4244

Hours: Open by appointment on
limited seasonal dates and limited
times. Otherwise closed

Guided and group tours: Available
for 15–30 people. Call for reservations

Facilities: Free parking

Size of garden: 20 acres

Recommended time for visit: 2 hrs.

No pets / No bicycles / Not wheel-
chair accessible

Seasonal highlights:
Spring: Native woodland
wildflowers
Fall: Fall foliage, late blooms

Nemours Mansion and Gardens

Rockland Road
P.O. Box 109
Wilmington, DE 19899

(302) 651-6912

Hours: Open May–November,
Tuesday–Sunday. Closed December–April, Mondays, Thanksgiving

Admission fees:
Adults & children over 16 only: $8

Guided and group tours:
Tuesday–Saturday, 9, 11, 1 and 3;
Sunday, 11, 1 and 3. Call for reserva-
tions

Facilities: Free parking, cafeteria at
Alfred I. du Pont Institute. Call
(302) 651-4740 for food service
information

Size of garden: 300 acres

Recommended time for visit: Guided
tours of Mansion and Gardens take
a minimum of 2 hrs.

No pets / No bicycles

Special events: Guided tours
of Mansion and Gardens May–
November

Seasonal highlights:
Spring: Bulbs
Summer: Herbaceous plants and
annuals
Fall: Fall color
Winter: Closed

Curator's choice: Colonnade,
Temple of Love, Sunken Garden

Pennsbury Manor

400 Pennsbury Memorial Road
Morrisville, PA 19067

(215) 946-0400

Hours: Tuesday–Saturday 9–5,
Sunday, 12–5. Closed Monday and
some holidays in fall and winter

Admission fees:
Adults: $5
Children ages 6–17: $3
Senior Citizens (65 and older): $4
Discounts for groups

Guided and group tours: Call for
reservations

Facilities: Free parking, gift shop,
handicap access, library specializing
in 17th-century life

Size of garden: area of special
interest is approximately 10 acres

Recommended time for visit: 2–3 hrs.

No pets / No bicycles

Special events: 80 special events and
programs throughout the year
April–October: Weekly living
history programs and monthly pre-
schooler workshops
Selected Saturday mornings: Garden
workshops
February: Hannah Penn Tea
March: Charter Day
May: Celebration of Spring
Summer eves: Picnics with music
September: Manor Fair
October: Annual Forum
December: Holly Night
Also, special school days, summer
camps, bus tours, seminars

Seasonal highlights:
Spring: Bulbs, herbaceous biennials
and perennials, and flowering
shrubs. Plantings of medicinal and
culinary herbs in Kitchen Garden
Summer: Kitchen Garden: vegetables, fruit, herbs; Upper Court:
container plantings
Fall: Fall vegetables

Curator's choice: The topiary and
container plants of the Upper
Court

Education: Classes for pre-school,
elementary school, high school
and adult

Pennsylvania Horticultural Society

325 Walnut Street
Philadelphia, PA 19106-2777

(215) 625-8250   *fax:* (215) 625-8288

Hours: Open: 9–5, Monday–Friday.
Closed: weekends/holidays

Admission fees: None

Facilities: Library, handicap access limited, access for strollers/baby carriages

Recommended time for visit: 1 hr.

No pets / No bicycles

Special events:
March: Philadelphia Flower Show
May: Azalea Garden Gala, Junior Flower Show
September: Harvest Show

Curator's choice: Library; 14,000 volumes (all horticulturally related). Lending privileges for members. Seed and nursery catalogs (for reference). Periodical subscriptions (for reference). Slide shows available for rent. Horticultural Hotline: (215) 922-8043

Education: Horticultural lectures, seminars, workshops, clinics, at-home programs, garden tours. PHS News and activities brochures mailed to members provide schedule of events

Other information: Small, 18th-century-style garden, maintained by members of the Society and part of the Independence National Historical Park

Pennsylvania Hospital Physic Garden

c/o Pennsylvania Hospital
9th & Pine Streets
Philadelphia, PA 19107

(215) 829-3971

Hours: Dawn to dusk year-round

Admission fees: None

Guided and group tours: Call for reservations

Facilities: Limited parking, gift shop (in the hospital), restaurant, picnicking, limited handicap access, library

Size of garden: a tennis court

Recommended time for visit: 45 min.

Special events:
April or May: Spring plant sale

Seasonal highlights:
Spring: Azaleas, wisteria, dogwood

Curator's choice: 18th-century medicinal plants; Franklinia

Pennypacker Mills

5 Haldeman Road
Schwenksville, PA 19473

(610) 287-9349

Hours: Tuesday–Saturday, 10–4;
Sunday, 1–4

Admission fees: By donation

Guided and group tours: Call for reservations

Facilities: Free parking, gift shop, picnicking, limited handicap access, library (by appointment only)

Size of garden: an estate of 125 acres

Recommended time for visit: 45 min.

Special events:
April: Springtime Celebration
May: Civil War Reunion
October: Halloween Celebration for children
December: Illuminated Open House

Seasonal highlights:
Winter: House decorated in Victorian style

Curator's choice: Garden landscaped in the English natural style

Education: Programs offered to groups

Peter Wentz Farmstead

Shearer Road and Route 73
Worcester, PA 19490

(610) 584-5104

Hours: Tuesday–Saturday 10–4.
Sunday 1–4. Last tour 3:30.
Closed Christmas, Easter, New Year's Day, 1st full week after Labor Day

Admission fees: Donations welcome

Guided and group tours: Available Tuesday–Sunday. Call for reservations

Facilities: Free parking, museum shop, decorative arts library

Size of garden: Historic farm with kitchen garden

Recommended time for visit: 1 hr.

No pets / Bicycles if walked on property

Special events:
June 1st: Muster Day
October 1st: Learenswaert

Seasonal highlights:
Spring: Planting of crops and spring maintenance
Summer: Flowers, harvest, seed-saving
Fall: Harvest, seed-saving, winter preparation

Curator's choice: The mansion at the farmstead

Schuylkill Center for Environmental Education

8480 Hagy's Mill Road
Philadelphia, PA 19128-9975

(215) 482-7300

Hours: 8:30–5 Monday–Saturday; Sunday, 1–5.
Bookstore 8:30–4:30 Monday–Saturday; Sunday 1–4:30.
Closed all major holidays; all Sundays in August

Admission fees:
Adults: $5
Children up to age 12: $3
Senior Citizens: $5
Students: $5
Discounts for groups: self-guided, $2 per person

Guided and group tours: Monday to Friday. Call for reservations

Facilities: Free parking, bookstore, handicap access, library

Recommended time for visit: 3 hrs.

No pets / No bicycles

Special events:
March: Founder's Day luncheon, environmental education awards
June: Walk with the Wild Things – pony rides, bluegrass band, games, contests, barbecue dinner
October: Fall Festival – games, pumpkin decorating, boat rides
December: Winter Festival – traditional lighting of the yule log

Seasonal highlights:
Spring: Wildflowers and tree flowers
Summer: Bird population and ponds
Fall: Fall foliage of upland forest plus bird migration
Winter: Spectacular view from Piedmont to Atlantic Coastal Plain and the City of Philadelphia

Curator's choice: View of downtown Philadelphia

Education: K–12 and graduate level studies

Scott Arboretum of Swarthmore College

500 College Avenue
Swarthmore, PA 19081-1397

(610) 328-8025

Hours: Dawn to dusk year-round. Office closed week of December 25, Thanksgiving and Friday after Thanksgiving, New Year's Day, July 4

Admission fees: None

Guided and group tours: For groups of 10 and over. Fee charged. Call for reservations

Facilities: Free parking, college bookstore, college snack bar, handicap access, library

Size of garden: 350-acre campus, collections concentrated on 110 acres

Special events:
January: Annual lecture/dinner
March–June: Spring schedule of educational events
May: Spring Festival, Garden Day tour on Mother's Day, even years
June: Garden Day Tour on Father's Day, odd years
September–December: Fall schedule of educational events
September: Plant sale – every other year in odd years
October: Fall Festival, perennials conference

Seasonal highlights:
Spring: Bulbs, lilacs, magnolias, cherries, rhododendrons and native azaleas, corylopsis, dogwoods, quince, crabapples
Summer: Rose garden, summer bloom garden, perennials and annuals, buddleias
Fall: Maples, viburnums, callicarpa – foliage and fruit interest, crabapples, hollies, a variety of grand specimen trees in fall color
Winter: Winter garden, hollies, witchhazels, pinetum, dwarf conifer collection

Curator's choice: For plantsmen – the holly collection (230 taxa) and tree peonies (54 taxa)
For designers – the Scott outdoor amphitheater; Fragrance garden; Teaching garden and Entrance garden; Harry Wood garden, Courtyard garden
For all – Wister Garden

Education: A variety of lectures, workshops, short courses, day trips and extended trips offered through the year

Stenton

4601 N. 18th Street
Philadelphia, PA 19140

(215) 329-7312

Hours: Open Tuesday–Saturday, 1–4; from January 1 – March 31, by appointment only

Admission fees:
Adults: $3
Children: $1.50
Senior Citizens: $2
Students: $2

Guided and group tours: Call for reservations

Facilities: Free parking, gift shop, picnicking (for a fee)

Size of garden: 1½ acres

Recommended time for visit: 1 hr.

No pets / No bicycles

Curator's choice: The Colonial Revival Garden

Swiss Pines

Charlestown Road
R.D. 1, Box 127
Malvern, PA

(610) 933-6916   *fax:* (610) 935-8795

Hours: Monday–Friday, 10–4, Saturday 9–12 noon
Closed: Sundays, holidays, any inclement weather or after heavy rain.
Closed December–May

Admission fees: Adults and children over 12: $5

Guided and group tours: Call for reservations

Facilities: Free parking

Size of garden: 8 acres

Recommended time for visit: 1 hr.

No children under 12 / No pets
No food / No buses

Curator's choice: This is a private Japanese garden designed for meditation

Taylor Memorial Arboretum

10 Ridley Drive
Wallingford, PA 19086-7256

(610) 876-2649

Hours: Open 9–4 daily. Closed major holidays

Admission fees: None

Guided and group tours: Occasionally

Facilities: Free parking, handicap access limited

Size of garden: 30 acres

Recommended time for visit: 1 hrs.

Pets on leash only / No bicycles
No food or beverages / No smoking / No radios or musical instruments

Seasonal highlights:
Spring: Toads mating; songbird migration; wildflowers, perennial garden, flowering trees, azaleas, rhododendrons, viburnums
Summer: Native species of *Leucothoe, clethra, Calycanthus*; perennials; floodplain meadow; *Franklinia alatamaha*
Fall: Dragonflies, fall songbird migration, perennials; fall color
Winter: Floodplain meadow, dried grasses, sedge meadow, witchhazels

Curator's choice: Giant dogwood (*Cornus controversa*); Disanthus (*Disanthus cercidifolius*); Rhododendron walk; Anne's Grotto; Bald Cypress pond; Azalea trail

Education: Classes in natural sciences and natural history, conservation biology, ecology, horticulture and related subjects offered to all age school groups

Temple University, Ambler Campus

580 Meetinghouse Road
Ambler, PA 19002–3999

(215) 283-1292

Hours: Open year-round

Admission fees: None

Guided and group tours: Call for reservations

Facilities: Free parking, restaurant, handicap access limited

Recommended time for visit: 30 min.

No pets

Special events: June Homecoming

Seasonal highlights:
Spring: Bulb display in woodland garden
Summer: Perennial borders in main garden
Fall: Perennial garden

Education: Credit classes in landscape architecture and horticulture. Also non-credit workshops

Tyler Arboretum

515 Painter Road
Media, PA 19063-4424

(610) 566-5431

Hours: Grounds open daily 8–dusk

Admission fees:
Adults: $3
Children 3–15: $1; under 3: free
Discounts for groups

Guided and group tours: Available weekdays 8:30–4 year-round. Call for reservations

Facilities: Free parking, gift shop, environmental education, library, handicap access in progress

Size of garden: 650 acres, of which 200 are cultivated

Recommended time for visit: 2–3 hrs.

Pets on leash / No bicycles

Special events:
January: Winter birdseed sale
February: Pancake breakfast; maple sugaring tours
April: Arbor Day Open House
May: Birdathon
June: Flea market (at Penn State Delco Campus); Tyler's Garden Gala (odd-numbered years only)
September: Plant sale (even-numbered years only)
October: Fall birdseed sale; Pumpkin Day Fall Festival

Seasonal highlights:
Spring: Rhododendron, lilac, crabapple, magnolia and cherry collections
Summer: Fragrant and butterfly gardens
Fall: Native trees
Winter: Pinetum and holly collections, bark park, winter aconites and snowdrops

Curator's choice: 150-year old trees planted by the founders of the site's original arboretum; several are state champions

Education: Educational programs available year-round for adults, children & families include teacher training, school tours, courses, lectures, guided walks & workshops

Wallingford Rose Garden

6 East Brookhaven Road
P.O. Box 52
Wallingford, PA 19086

(610) 566-2110

Hours: Open by appointment only

Admission fees: None

Guided and group tours: Call for reservations

Facilities: Free parking, handicap access limited

Size of garden: 3 acres

Recommended time for visit: 1 hr. minimum

No pets / No bicycles

Special events:
May: Plant sale
June: Rose garden walks
November–December: Holly collection walks

Seasonal highlights:
Spring: Rhododendron, dogwood, other flowering trees
Summer: Roses in early June; cactus in containers' area
Fall: Roses
Winter: Holly collection

Curator's choice: Holly cathedral; dawn redwoods; rose garden, wall of climbing roses

Winterthur Museum, Garden, Library

Winterthur
Delaware 19735

(302) 888-4600 *or* (800) 448-3883
TTY: (302) 888-4907

Hours: Monday–Saturday, 9–5; Sunday 12–5. Closed January 1, Thanksgiving Day, Christmas Day

Admission fees:
Adults: $8
Guild Members: free
Age 5–11: $4
Senior Citizens: $6
Students: $6
Group Discounts: 20 or more, $6

Guided and group tours: Museum tours, unreserved and reserved. Please phone for information. Garden tram tours, narrated, year-round. Free with General Admission. Free to Guild Members

Facilities: Free parking, gift shops, restaurant (you are welcome to shop and dine at Winterthur without an admission ticket), picnicking, handicap access, library specializing in American decorative arts, plus books on horticulture and garden design

Size of garden: 980 acres (60 landscaped acres)

Recommended time for visit: 1 hr. minimum for garden, several hours for museum plus garden

No pets / No bicycles

Special events:
March or April: Easter Sunday
May: Point-to-Point
July: County Pride Pops Concert
November–December: Yuletide at Winterthur (Museum tour)

Seasonal highlights:
Spring: March Bank (early spring bulbs); Winter-hazel walk (early April); Quince walk, Sargent Cherries, daffodils, Sundial garden, flowering shrubs (April); Azalea Woods (early May); Quarry gar-

den, primulas (May and June); Peony garden (May)
Summer: Reflecting pool and Glade garden; Sycamore area (summer blooming shrubs); Quarry garden; rhododendron maximum, Cornus kousa, Philadelphus (June); native azaleas, shrub roses, hosta
Fall: Views and vistas in autumn coloring; colchicum; callicarpa in fruit; viburnum in fruit
Winter: Snow scenes; pinetum; witchhazel; Snowdrops; Adonis amurensis (late winter); Eranthus hyemalis (late winter)

Curator's choice: Azalea Woods in early May; Sundial garden in late April; views from Bristol Summer House and Oak Hill; Davidia involucrata—one of the best specimens in the U.S.; Sargent Cherries

Education: Graduate studies in Early American Civilization and Culture and Art Conservation, given in conjunction with the University of Delaware. Also lectures, seminars, conferences

Wyck

6026 Germantown Avenue
Philadelphia, PA 19144

(215) 848-1690

Hours: April 1–December 15, Tuesday, Thursday, Saturday 1–4 pm, and year-round by appointment. Closed Sundays and major holidays

Admission fees:
Adults: $3
Children up to age 12: $1
Senior Citizens: $2
Students: $2
No discounts for groups

Guided and group tours: Available Monday–Saturday, 9:30–4. Call for reservations

Facilities: Free parking, gift shop, handicap access limited, library specializing in horticulture and botany from 1770 to 1970

Size of garden: 2½ acres

Recommended time for visit: 1 hr. for house and garden. 30 min. garden only

No pets / No bicycles

Special events:
April: Spring lecture
April–November: Garden Playdays for children by appointment
June: Old Rose Garden – Open House
October: Wyck-Strickland Award Dinner
December: Holiday tours

Seasonal highlights:
Spring: Flowering shrubs, tree peonies
Summer: Roses, vegetable garden
Fall: Trees
Winter: Winter jasmine

Curator's choice: Old Rose Garden growing in its original plan with its original varieties since the 1820s

Education: Workshops, lectures

Zoological Society of Philadelphia

34th Street & Girard Avenue
Philadelphia, PA 19104

(215) 243-1100

Hours: 9:30–5 daily. Closed
Thanksgiving, Christmas Eve,
Christmas Day, New Year's Eve,
New Year's Day

Admission fees:
Adults: $8
Children: Age 2–11 $5.50
(under 2 free)
Senior Citizens: $5.50
Discounts for group

Group tours available: Call for
reservations

Facilities: Parking ($4; members
free), gift shop, restaurant, picnicking, handicap access

Size of garden: 42 acres

Recommended time for visit:
Minimum 2 hrs.

No pets / No bicycles

Special events:
February: Valentine's Day Event;
Purim Festival
March: Flower Show of Civic
Center
April: Garden Gear Up (volunteer
zoo cleanup); Volunteer Gala
(National Recognition Month)
May: Conservation Festival;
Zoobilee (dinner dance fund raiser)
June: African-American Culture
Fest
July: Razzle/Dazzle
July & August: Radio Promotions
September: Adopt Day
October: Boo at the Zoo
November: A–Z Run

Seasonal highlights:
Spring: Featured animal exhibit,
flowering trees, camel and pony
rides, wildlife theater, children's
zoo programs
Summer: Backyard bugs exhibit
Fall: Changing of season
Winter: Peaceful

Curator's choice: Spring display of
flowering shrubs and trees

Education: Activity oriented workshops on a variety of animal conservation related topics for 2–12 year-
olds. Most classes are 1–2 hours in
length and include live animals in
the classroom. Workshops are ad-
vertised in a quarterly members'
newsletter

Selected References

A Short History of Botany in the United States. ed. Joseph Ewan. New York: Hafner Publishing Co., 1969.

Allman, Herbert D. *A Unique Institution: The Story of the National Farm School*. Philadelphia: Jewish Publication Society of America, 1935.

America's Garden Legacy: A Taste of Pleasure. ed. George H. M. Lawrence. Philadelphia: The Pennsylvania Horticultural Society, 1978.

Baatz, Simon. *"Venerate The Plough": A History of the Philadelphia Society for Promoting Agriculture, 1785-1985*. Philadelphia: PSPA, 1985.

Baltzell, E. Digby. *Puritan Boston and Quaker Philadelphia: Two Protestant Ethics and the Spirit of Class Authority and Leadership*. New York: The Free Press, Macmillan Publishing Co., 1979.

———. *Philadelphia Gentlemen: The Making of a National Upper Class*. Philadelphia: University of Pennsylvania Press, 1979.

Bartram, William. *Travels Through North & South Carolina, Georgia, East & West Florida, the Cherokee Country, the Extensive Territories of the Muscogulges, or Creek Confederacy, and the Country of the Chactaws; Containing an Account of the Soil and Natural Productions of Those Regions, Together with Observations of the Manners of the Indians*. Philadelphia, 1791.

Blood, William. *Apostle of Reason: A Biography of Joseph Krauskopf*. Philadelphia: Dorrance and Company, 1973.

Braun, E. Lucy. *Deciduous Forests of Eastern North America*. Philadelphia: The Blakiston Co., 1950.

Bridenbaugh, Carl. *Cities in the Wilderness: The First Century of Urban Life in America, 1625–1742*. London: Oxford University Press, 1966.

Brownlee, David B. *Building the City Beautiful: The Benjamin Franklin Parkway and the Philadelphia Museum of Art*. Philadelphia: Philadelphia Museum of Art, 1989.

Bruce, Hal. *Winterthur in Bloom: Winter, Spring, Summer, Autumn*. Winterthur, Delaware: Winterthur Books, 1968.

Buist, Robert. *American Flower-Garden Directory*. New York: Orange Judd & Company, 1854.

Burt, Nathaniel. *The Perennial Philadelphians: The Anatomy of an American Aristocracy*. Boston: Little, Brown and Co., 1963.

Bush-Brown, Louise, and James Bush-Brown. *Portraits of Philadelphia Gardens*. Philadelphia: Dorrance and Company, 1929.

Canby, Henry Seidel. *The Brandywine*. West Chester, Pennsylvania: Schiffer Publishing, Ltd., 1941.

Clark, Kenneth. *Landscape Into Art*. London: John Murray, 1976.

Contosta, David R. *A Philadelphia Family: The Houstons and Woodwards of Chestnut Hill*. Philadelphia: University of Pennsylvania Press, 1988.

Correspondence between William Penn and James Logan. ed. Edward Armstrong. New York: AMS Press, Historical Society of Pennsylvania, reprinted 1973.

Doell, Gerald Allan, and M. Christine Klim Doell. *Pennypacker Mill: Landscape History and Preliminary Master Plan*. Cortland, New York: Doell and Doell, 1983.

Downing, Andrew Jackson. *A Treatise on the Theory and Practice of Landscape Gardening adapted to North America with a view to the Improvement of Country Residences*. New York: Wiley and Putnam, 1844.

Eberlein, Harold Donaldson. *Portrait of a Colonial City: Philadelphia, 1670–1838*. Philadelphia: J. B. Lippincott Company, 1939.

1876, A Centennial Exhibition. ed. Robert Post. Washington, D.C.: Smithsonian, National Museum of History and Technology, 1974.

Engdahl, Bonnie. *Paradise in the New World: A Study of the Image of the Garden in the Literature*. University of California, Los Angeles, Ph.D., 1967; Ann Arbor, Michigan: University Microfilms, Inc.

Faris, John T. *Old Gardens in and about Philadelphia and those who made them*. Indianapolis: The Bobbs-Merrill Company, 1932.

Favretti, Rudy J., and Joy Putman Favretti. *Landscapes and Gardens for Historic Buildings: A handbook for reproducing and creating authentic landscape settings*. Nashville: American Association for State and Local History, 1978.

Fox, Stephen. *The American Conservation Movement: John Muir and his legacy*. Madison: The University of Wisconsin Press, 1985.

From Seed to Flower: Philadelphia 1681-1876, A Horticultural Point of View. ed. The Library Committee. Philadelphia: The Pennsylvania Horticultural Society, 1976.

Gardens & Arboreta of Philadelphia and the Delaware Valley. ed. The Tercentenary Gardens Collaborative Editorial Board. Philadelphia: Morris Arboretum of the University of Pennsylvania, 1981.

Gardens: Architectural Digest. ed. Paige Rense. Los Angeles: The Knapp Press, 1983.

Gardens of the World; The Art and Practice of Gardening. eds. Penelope Hobhouse and Elvin McDonald. New York: Macmillan Publishing Co., 1991.

Gavan, Anthony N. B. "Proprietary Philadelphia as Artifact." In *The Historian and the City*. ed. Oscar Handlin and John Burchard. Cambridge: MIT Press, 1963.

Giamatti, A. Bartlett. *The Earthly Paradise and the Renaissance Epic*. New York: W. W. Norton & Co., 1966.

Gibson, Jane Mork. *The Fairmount Waterworks*. Bulletin of the Philadelphia Museum of Art: Volume 84, Numbers 360, 361, 1988.

Greenfeld, Howard. *The Devil and Dr. Barnes: Portrait of an American Art Collector*. New York: Viking Penguin Inc., 1987.

Greiff, Constance M. *Independence: The Creation of a National Park*. Philadelphia: University of Pennsylvania Press, 1987.

Hadfield, Miles. *A History of British Gardening*. London: John Murray Ltd., 1979.

Hall, J. Hudson. *Archeology at the Highlands: Social Stratification and the Egalitarian Ideal in Whitemarsh, 1795–1850*. Philadelphia: University of Pennsylvania, dissertation, 1978.

Hazelhurst, F. Hamilton. *Gardens of Illusion: The Genius of Andre LeNotre*. Nashville: Vanderbilt University Press, 1980.

Hedrick, Ulysses Prentiss. *A History of Horticulture in America to 1860*. New York: Oxford University Press, 1950.

Hinde, Thomas. *Capability Brown: The Story of a Master Gardener*. London: Century Hutchinson Ltd., 1986.

Hughes, Thomas P. *American Genesis: A Century of Invention and Technological Enthusiasm, 1870–1970*. New York: Penguin Books, 1989.

Hunt, John Dixon. *Gardens and the Picturesque: Studies in the History of Landscape Architecture*. Cambridge, Massachusetts: The MIT Press, 1992.

Hunt, Rachel McMasters Miller. *William Penn Horticulturist*. Pittsburgh, Pennsylvania: University of Pittsburgh Press, 1953.

Hyams, Edward. *Capability Brown & Humphry Repton*. New York: Charles Scribner's Sons, 1971.

Jackson, John Brinkerhoff. *American Space: The Centennial Years 1865–1876*. New York: W. W. Norton & Co., Inc., 1972.

———. *Discovering the Vernacular Landscape*. New Haven: Yale University Press, 1984.

James, Marquis. *Alfred I. du Pont: The Family Rebel*. New York: The Bobbs-Merrill Company, 1941.

Jellett, Edwin. *Germantown Gardens and Gardeners*. Philadelphia: H. F. McCann, 1914.

John & William Bartram's America; Selections from the Writings of the Philadelphia Naturalists. ed. Helen Gere Cruickshank. New York: The Devin-Adair Company, 1957.

Kammen, Michael. *A Machine That Would Go of Itself: The Constitution in American Culture*. New York: Vintage Books, 1987.

Kaplan, Rachel, and Stephen Kaplan. *The Experience of Nature: A Psychological Perspective*. New York: Cambridge University Press, 1989.

Kastner, Joseph. *A Species of Eternity*. New York: Alfred A. Knopf, Inc., 1977.

Klein, Esther. *Fairmount Park: A History and A Guidebook*. Bryn Mawr: Harcum Junior College Press, 1974.

Leighton, Ann. *American Gardens of the Nineteenth Century: For Comfort and Affluence*. Amherst: The University of Massachusetts Press, 1987.

Letters from an American Farmer and Sketches of Eighteenth-Century America by J. Hector St. John de Crevecoeur. ed. Albert E. Stone. New York: Viking Penguin Books, 1981.

Lukacs, John A. *Philadelphia, Patricians & Philistines, 1900–1950*. New York: Farrar-Straus-Giroux, 1980.

Malone, Dumas. *The Sage of Monticello*. Boston: Little, Brown and Co., 1981.

Marx, Leo. *The Machine in the Garden: Technology and the Pastoral Ideal in America*. New York: Oxford University Press, 1964.

Master Plan: The Tinicum National Environmental Center. Newton Corner, Massachusetts: United States Department of the Interior Fish and Wildlife Service, 1983.

McCabe, James D. *The Illustrated History of the Centennial Exhibition; held in commemoration of the one hundredth anniversary of American Independence*. Philadelphia: National Publishing Co., collector's reprint, 1975.

McCormick, Jack. *An Ecological Inventory of the West Park, Fairmount Park, City of Philadelphia*. Report by Jack McCormick Associates, 1971.

McHarg, Ian L. *Design with Nature*. Garden City, New York: The Natural History Press, 1969.

McLean, Elizabeth. "Town and Country Gardens in Eighteenth-Century Philadelphia" in *British and American Gardens in the Eighteenth Century; eighteen illustrated essays on garden history*. ed. Robert P. Maccubbin and Peter Martin. Williamsburg, Virginia: The Colonial Williamsburg Foundation, 1984.

Moore, Charles W., William J. Mitchell and William Turnbull, Jr. *The Poetics of Gardens*. Cambridge, Massachusetts: The MIT Press, 1988.

Nash, Roderick. *Wilderness and the American Mind*. New Haven: Yale University Press, 1982.

Nicholson, Philippa. *V. Sackville-West's Garden Book*. London: Michael Joseph, 1968.

Page, Russell. *The Education of a Gardener*. London: Collins, 1962.

Penn, William. *Fruits of Solitude*. London: Friends United, 1693.

Peter Kalm's Travels in North America; 1753. ed. Adolph B. Benson. New York: Dover Publications, Inc., reprinted 1966.

Philadelphia: A 300-Year History. ed. Russell F. Weigley. New York: W. W. Norton & Company for the Barra Foundation, 1982.

Philadelphia Merchant: The Diary of Thomas P. Cope, 1800–1851. ed. Eliza Cope Harrison. South Bend, Indiana: Gateway Editions, Ltd., 1978.

Pinchot, Gifford. *Breaking New Ground*. Washington, D.C.: Island Press, 1974.

Pollan, Michael. *Second Nature: A gardener's education*. New York: The Atlantic Monthly Press, 1991.

Postman, Neil. *Technopoly: The Surrender of Culture to Technology*. New York: Random House, Inc., 1993.

Prest, John. *The Garden of Eden: The Botanic Garden and the Re-Creation of Paradise*. New Haven: Yale University Press, 1981.

Prophet With Honor: The Career of Andrew Jackson Downing, 1815–1852. ed. George B. Tatum and Elisabeth Blair MacDougall. Washington, D.C.: Dumbarton Oaks, 1989.

Randall, Colvin. *Longwood Gardens: The Ultimate Garden Treasure*. Kennett Square, Pennsylvania: Longwood Gardens, Inc., 1987.

Remember William Penn, 1644–1944, A Tercentenary Memorial. ed. The William Penn Tercentenary Committee. Harrisburg, Pennsylvania: Pennsylvania Historical Commission, 1944.

Rivinus, Marion W. *Lights Along the Schuylkill*. Philadelphia: Rivinus, 1967.

Rivinus, Marion and Katharine Hansell Biddle. *Lights Along the Delaware*. Philadelphia: Dorrance and Company, Ltd., 1965.

Roberts, George and Mary Roberts. *Triumph on Fairmount: Fiske Kimball and the Philadelphia Museum of Art*. Philadelphia, 1959.

Roper, Laura Wood. *FLO: A Biography of Frederick Law Olmsted*. Baltimore: The John Hopkins University Press, 1973.

Rosenberg, David. *The Lost Book of Paradise; Adam and Eve in the Garden of Eden*. New York: Hyperion, 1993.

Scott, Frank J. *The Art of Beautifying Suburban Home Grounds*. Watkins Glen, New York: Library of Victorian Culture, American Life Foundation, 1982.

Scully, Vincent. *Architecture: The Natural and the Manmade*. New York: St. Martin's Press, 1991.

Sedgwick, John. *The Peaceable Kingdom: A Year in the Life of America's Oldest Zoo*. New York: William Morrow and Co., Inc., 1988.

Seebohm, Caroline, and Christopher Simon Sykes. *Private Landscapes; Creating Form, Vistas, and Mystery in the Garden*. New York: Clarkson N. Potter, Inc., 1989.

Shepard, Paul. *Man in the Landscape: A Historic View of the Esthetics of Nature*. College Station, Texas: Texas A&M University Press, 1991.

"Shepheard, Sir Peter." In *Reflections on Landscape: The lives and work of six British landscape architects.* ed. Sheila Harvey. Brookfield, Vermont: Gower Publishing Co., 1987.

Spirn, Anne Whiston. *The Granite Garden: Urban Design and Human Design.* New York: Basic Books, Inc., 1984.

Stokes, Charlotte C. *Documentation of the Victorian Gardens at the Maxwell Mansion.* Philadelphia: Ebenezer Maxwell Inc., 1981.

Sweeney, John A. H. *Henry Francis du Pont: Observations on the occasion of the 100th anniversary of his birth.* May 27, 1980.

Thacker, Christopher. *The History of Gardens.* Berkeley, California: University of California Press, 1979.

The Genius of the Place: The English Landscape Garden 1620–1820. ed. John Dixon Hunt and Peter Willis. Cambridge, Massachusetts: The MIT Press, 1988.

The Meaning of Gardens: Idea, Place, and Action. ed. Mark Francis and Randolph T. Hester, Jr. Cambridge, Massachusetts: The MIT Press, 1990.

The Spirit and the Intellect: Haverford College, 1833–1983. ed. Gregory Kannerstein. Haverford, Pennsylvania: Haverford College, 1983.

The Wilderness World of John Muir. ed. Edwin Way Teale. Boston: Houghton Mifflin Co., 1954.

Thomas Jefferson's Garden Book, 1766–1824, With relevant extracts from his other writings. annot. Edwin Morris Betts. Philadelphia: Memoirs of the American Philosophical Society, reprinted 1992.

Thompson, Sr., George E. *A Man and his Garden: The Story of Pierre S. du Pont's Development of Longwood Gardens.* Kennett Square, Pennsylvania: Longwood Gardens, Inc., 1976.

Tinkcom, Harry M., Margaret B. Tinkcom and Grant Miles Simon. *Historic Germantown.* Philadelphia: American Philosophical Society, 1955.

Wainwright, Nicholas B. *Andalusia: Countryseat of the Craig Family and of Nicholas Biddle and his descendents.* Philadelphia: The Historical Society of Pennsylvania, 1976.

Wallace, Paul A.W. *Indians in Pennsylvania.* 2nd ed. revised by William A. Hunter. Harrisburg: Pennsylvania Historical and Museum Commission, 1981.

Wallace Roberts & Todd. *Fairmount Park; Masterplan—Summary.* Philadelphia: The Fairmount Park Commission, 1983.

———. *A Landscape Plan for Haverford College.* Philadelphia: Haverford College, 1984.

Weygandt, Cornelius. *Philadelphia Folks: Ways and Institutions in and about the Quaker City.* New York: D. Appleton-Century Co., 1938.

White, Theophilus B. *Fairmount, Philadelphia's Park a history.* Philadelphia: Philadelphia Art Alliance Press, 1975.

Whyte, William H. *The Last Landscape.* New York: Doubleday & Co., Inc., 1968.

———. *The Social Life of Small Urban Places.* Washington: The Conservation Foundation, 1980.

Wicker, Alan. *An Introduction to Ecological Psychology.* Monterey: Brooks/Cole Publishing Co., 1979.

Wilson, Edward O. *The Diversity of Life.* Cambridge: The Belknap Press of Harvard University, 1992

Wilkinson, Norman B. *E. I. du Pont, Botaniste: The Beginning of a Tradition.* Charlottesville: The University Press of Virginia, 1972.

Wolf, Edwin II. *Philadelphia, Portrait of an American City: A Bicentennial History.* Harrisburg: Stackpole Books, 1975.

NOTE: *Brochures, calendars and unpublished materials for each of the gardens were generously shared. Copies of some of this material along with research notes are on file in the archives of the Morris Arboretum of the University of Pennsylvania.*

Index

NOTE: *Plants have been given their Latin names and appear in italics. Page numbers in italics refer to illustrations.*

Author
WILLIAM M. KLEIN, JR.

Photography
DEREK FELL

Manuscript editor
CAROLINE SEEBOHM

Production director
CHARLES AULT

Publisher
DAVID BARTLETT

Book design
CHRISTOPHER KUNTZE

Production editor
FREEMAN KEITH

Composition
PASSUMPSIC PUBLISHING

Map design
DIANA SHANNON

Stamping art
JON LUOMA

Printing
FRIESEN PRESS

This book was composed in Galliard, Meta, and Centaur types. It was printed in an edition of 10,000 copies. The binding cloth is Scholco Brillianta.

Date Due

All library items are subject to recall at any time.